kybyz

John Comeau

revision date: 2025-07-13 11:46:43 -0700, commit fbc57f6

Contents

Chapter 1

kybyz

a peer to peer collaboration and social media platform

intended to be a replacement for, among others:

- Facebook
- Twitter/X
- Messenger
- Calendar
- To-do lists

also meant to re-envision, or improve upon:

- Charles Cameron[1]'s hipbone games and analysis tools
- curating, and providing human-readable and memorable titles for, IPFS[2] content
- delivery services like DoorDash and `https://w-a-s-t-e.org/`
- rideshare services like Uber and Lyft
- online identity, proof of age, and document signing

if kybyz can incorporate web3 (decentralized finance) functionality, it will also be able to revolutionize such things as:

- auction sites like ebay
- escrow services
- freelancing sites like Upwork and Toptal

1.1 quickstart

Install and test on a `https://digitalocean.com` Debian-11 droplet, the cheapest one, currently $6/month.

NOTE if these instructions do not work, revert to the same version as the README. You will be missing the latest functionality, but the steps have a better chance of working correctly. I don't test the installation often.

Also: in the following, `RH` means RedHat-based distros, such as CentOS and Rocky Linux.

1. Login as root
2. `apt update` (RH: use `yum`)
3. `apt upgrade`
4. `apt install make git xauth` (RH: + `gcc firefox python3-devel`)

[1] `https://zenpundit.com/?p=68207`
[2] `https://ipfs.tech/`

5. `adduser tester`
6. `usermod -a -G sudo tester` (will be `sudoers` on some systems)
7. `mkdir ~tester/.ssh`
8. `cp ~/.ssh/authorized_keys ~tester/.ssh/`
9. `chown -R tester.tester ~tester/.ssh`

That's all as root; you should now login as a regular user

1. Login as tester; use `ssh -X` to tunnel Xwindows to your local box
2. Set `KB_USERNAME=myusername` and `KB_EMAIL=myemail@example.com`, replacing `myusername` and `myemail@example.com` with your own, hopefully unique, username and your real email address.
3. `gpg \ -default-new-key-algo "rsa3072/cert,sign+rsa3072/encr" \ -pinentry-mode loopback \ -quick-gen-key "$KB_USERNAME <$KB_EMAIL>" \ default default never` (just hit the enter key at the `Passphrase:` prompt)
4. `mkdir -p src`
5. `cd src`
6. `git clone https://github.com/jcomeauictx/kybyz`
7. `cd kybyz`
8. `cp Makefile.template Makefile`, and edit Makefile with your `KB_USERNAME` and `KB_EMAIL` values.
9. `sudo make install && make install` (CS: `sudo make install` will fail and you'll need to `make install` separately.)
10. `make` (Wait until the browser launches and you see a cat netmeme. There should be a `kbz>` prompt. If not, wait a few seconds and hit the enter key, and it should appear. **If pylint fails**, you can still test the app using `make PYLINT=echo`
11. Wait for the `kbz>` prompt
12. `send myusername myemail@example.com this is a private message` (remember to use your actual kybyz username and email)
13. Watch the log messages and make sure it was sent and received correctly.
14. Send to another online user. First you'll need to import their public GPG key (kybyzdotcom public key is below in this README; copy and paste it into a plain text file, and name it kybyzdotcom.pub).
15. ^C to get back to the command line.
16. `gpg -import kybyzdotcom.pub`
17. `gpg -sign-key kybyzdotcom`
18. `make`
19. At the `kbz>` prompt: `send kybyzdotcom kybyz@kybyz.com hey this is Joe`

If kybyzdotcom is online, he'll be able to read your message, but won't be able to verify who it's from unless he has imported *your* key.

1.2 troubleshooting

Testing while chrooting to different debootstrapped systems reveals some problems. I already mentioned pylint: if the version is too old, it will complain about many non-problems in the code. For that, just set PYLINT=echo preceding the `make` command.

If the version of gpg is too old, it will create empty `$HOME/.gnupg/secring.gpg` and `$HOME/.gnupg/pubring.gpg` files and break your current gpg setup. In that case:

- Remove those two files
- `mkdir -m 0700 $HOME/.gnupg_v1`
- Make sure /usr/local/bin precedes /usr/bin in your PATH; You can fix this in your `$HOME/.bashrc` or `.bash_aliases` files.
- Create, with mode 755, a file `/usr/local/bin/gpg` with the following contents: `bash #!/bin/bash /usr/bin/gpg -homedir $HOME/.gnupg_v1 "$@"`
- `gpg -gen-key`, and follow the prompts.

If you're helping alpha test, each day before running the script you should `git pull`. This brings in any code changes since the previous attempt.

If you imported the expired kybyzdotcom public key (before 2024-12-29), you should be able to get the new one using `gpg -refresh-keys`. It seemed to work automagically for me, anyway. Then when signing with `gpg -sign-key`, I had to use the entire 40-character ID, instead of "kybyzdotcom", to be able to sign the new key: `gpg -sign-key 341764CDFD52C18832E29A39110861CDBFA29713`

1.3 proof of authorship

On a platform such as Facebook, proof of authorship is "automatic" in the sense that, on a centralized platform, everyone has a unique ID protected by their password. Of course, passwords can be guessed, phished, or otherwise obtained by other people and thus can impersonate the author, but generally speaking, if you see a post from jcomeauictx, you can assume I was the author.

On a peer to peer system it's a lot harder. We'll be using cryptographic signatures with gpg (GNU's implementation of Pretty Good Privacy, PGP), but you'll still have to get your public key out to the people you want in your network using: `gpg -armor -export me@example.com | \ mail -s "my public key" myfriend@example.com`

1.4 timestamping

In addition to proof of authorship, we will need to have a provable timestamp, not just the falsifiable "timestamp" field currently in example.kybyz/netmeme.json. See `https://www.jamieweb.net/blog/proof-of-timestamp/` for some ideas on this; for example, you can embed the hash of the post in a BCH transaction along with the hash of the previous block. This proves the post is no older than the previous block, and no newer than the transaction timestamp.

There is now a somewhat-decentralized service for this: `https://opentimestamps.org/`

1.5 prerequisites

- python3
- gpg

1.6 notes on Android

It can run under Termux. Install from f-droid, not from the App Store. You will need to install a number of packages, including `python`, `uwsgi`, and many others I can't think of at the moment. And with `pip`, you will have to get, at least, `pylint`.

Termux has the uwsgi package, but no plugin for Python, so we must build one.

1. `git clone https://github.com/jcomeauictx/uwsgi` at the Termux shell prompt, and cd to the directory
2. Find what version of uwsgi you have; `uwsgi -version`. I had 2.0.20
3. Check out that version into its own branch: `git checkout tags/2.0.20 -bv2.0.20`
4. `PYTHON=python3 uwsgi -build-plugin "plugins/python python3"`
5. `cd ../kybyz`; and `ln -s ../uwsgi/python3_plugin.so .`
6. `make`

1.7 kybyzdotcom public key

"' —–BEGIN PGP PUBLIC KEY BLOCK—–

mQGNBGdxuEQBDADEfYr7yLL8+iedd9rZtJmCZ7k2KJCd3R5CkPTJdD5rhQURh+yp
v5bWkoqLAwWUk1IH7Q2iW5/e8cued/GCBv4Z720JKdhQmq3vs7pxiEZtWc4B79PW
HpQcbYb7ouJXwM16b2GcET2vn9xMaUeVbpePiAr5OiRiLZjDceevzjWyqq/MQlXz
zfct1vbWwlqJml2mvuIsvhuSEpf0zOUqJ6Xlo7unDQ8TtlVEA2YpBSU0IX8tdpal
U1ecVBw5Q9BiDHqepca+w3IwRL9+4zJl3eKvfKLTo8VoMxxyanBizrGQaofBCIGb
qTxOtSGjJggx+5eAs3k/Qxy88f5RSTtk53QODzj1txSe2GWsnahO/t0ABrcAQXgd
t13+ifFQ1F4eli0DtThtwMkhA00QKmvU7F7BX8BvDbjKatRT3OgwVhCQfGYg9G9t
5+cGvCXPlEwl7J6Yvwze4ysJemYAYjLk+5pxLUpmQK55XjGZgXEQfbbupoWYKXzX
cazQC9CkSZnf+58AEQEAAbQda3lieXpkb3Rjb20gPGt5Ynl6QGt5Ynl6LmNvbT6J
Ac4EEwEKADgWIQQ0F2TN/VLBiDLimjkRCGHNv6KXEwUCZ3G4RAIbAwULCQgHAgYV
CgkICwIEFgIDAQIeAQIXgAAKCRARCGHNv6KXE9zsC/9uiYHfsJFEGSFNTf1l/xKP
OXVhBYgvoGR/1ejsSOOtx34B8SJicGlCBzNvdZc5tO6DUs5Uvghosjlje3ZDPeBs
kN5rM755Fe9yBBxxNrqRGuwknzd2vScnrEJ5kMSsZ385myP+USeOVTaiPP8bqXUA
JnXtYZ2wrOJx8ctj7MDdYW1bx2wrgX+yfE1j+STBhhOTZhoTDRMblW6OIegriRp/
8L5O5OvJ9b+4tEjYiki8lBIresL/vjNlL1hJLE7Wq3jcwdmpySZz4zJic+nuu0hZ
Olv3oB5zou2GxjN1Bbo7BfT11PZtycMXRblOkRxx0iWGRNwwPpgVx5DWeuPmVgaa
AHNEjkGPxdn6kSMJDZ99V+wCG5mkBF1+0+nhvHq4B7nGiAkrI9UZpCiOCq1N82TI
pArytHjOxl1THb6B8/ALCyv0Lt8A0hwSV6eSmaKUOa0B45fTCy7VN59YdMuUzIlK
kbqnkRAA0t8BdnqW+lVuO2T9xy4qZU1bvM90Jz87Za65AY0EZ3G4RAEMAL/FAnQM
B0RwAkBA1zZMpXRFxDqUUprxre8P0HE7NAtKSsIujLj+UxX/5Sl3AMEEmG+bD7q2
OJV9lr80O+vEWg4rKd4WQF6QYrCc6Ya+4O8a/aILHAhPqUOlJVAVG7a70u5LQahR
mzq4YLVbwpMGBcDGGsOKfho350wfQCSURVIhg2HsbtPoCIRz1N8q0ljwP3YtTwNX
7rR44hyOoPdukTyM4JnNBa8tNXxuHJ2aycAWSCQ7/2VmOfOMcKWjb6yWIARu6iaY
PE6V63FiQ+7gSE0EWcqD+ITETGhV+o9GZaG2yOY4f7fB4E1qXqlxGB4R5aYq9xiY
992jS9SH0mBxL4RjLoTia81W6GHi5RQ9mlo8wNtMlnQmItL4FWVZ4g3WjmfpcOwX
i+8lOePwiySx8txne/w/JLyxVcK2TiLqqCpZCef+tAndeA00YgK4GWZqqAqf6KfG LMn-
nWgk86jfm1CZj+VkyULbiFX/8VnI6whqznYuAAi9+4vFYa1IdBoDB4wARAQAB
iQG2BBgBCgAgFiEENBdkzf1SwYgy4po5EQhhzb+ilxMFAmdxuEQCGwwACgkQEQhh
zb+ilxPhUgwAw8UZZCw7lmLI8jhHMeKwHuVdd6D0/3tggO6C3VSCcxtnLDf1645m
mVtK+Mdaj0I0yrRe5i3yiXuJowVT0JIlDyXc+qg6t8phGVeMv/edJ5Ha56HwQbbK
18DThb9CM2bXMXYnPSMYUI1A103Pz7+IPCP/Zk6wRtRF+UpuKz23180XM3RqvppZ
DIweqyqSl9+5/dTMtdxyvPjmubGEpIDgZ2TlPEg2vhbgts0Cy4Ux22cPYONOuuYq yGc-
qLHinhN9SMdLenLWxqNXwmouDaNk+auD/64BeDR7kgJTOTxzOHgsBoA0cOYRA
W1VwSVtxdsNAZJOdP29mwnf/Q/SE/VJLj/+Rb8xv90uFD4yZgMJ4IFSv6nx4AOTh
eXTwkj4agFx1a7Gm4raH11hTqU00dOmNSIgVbABtbC9xonSS8opCkivs1FInVJqf
Ct5b/6KeJsXHF2wRKjzBNNej9V8kjjF5OQhQcgYTWujgfe8PcHO3E9adJYPmjLnb SnaMYEGiKugA
=LueN ---END PGP PUBLIC KEY BLOCK---

1.8 file storage considerations

using the filesystem as database, at least until I figure out how kybyz is supposed to work. some random thoughts:

- use file ownership for friends' posts: requires `sudo adduser` to friend someone. must add `kybyz` user and group, and add all friends to `kybyz` group.
- use `nobody` (add `kybyz` group to it) for not-yet-friended others' posts.
- subdirectories of `$HOME/.kybyz` for friends, topics, etc.
- file extensions for different types of posts?
- one subdirectory for storage (named `storage`?) for all files, symlinking to other subdirectories as needed?
- split hashes into chunks of 2 or 4 in order to keep inodes per directory optimized for fast retrieval? or just use ext4 or xfs and not worry about it? e.g. `storage/fe/e3/44/2a/fee3442a.txt`

"‘

Chapter 2

developer notes

- Cloudflare, which is used (now, anyway) by ipfs.io, is returning 403 "Forbidden" errors on urllib requests[1]. need to change useragent string. (fixed by commit 6903a329df)
- debugging messages are not shown in console window; the debug log is located at `$HOME/.local/log/kybyz.log`
- `https://uwsgi-docs.readthedocs.io/en/latest/WSGIquickstart.html`
- Heit suggested WebRTC for p2p communication[2]
- on iphone6 iSH, uwsgi gives error "unable to set PTHREAD*PRIO*INHERIT"
- need to come up with canonical way to list resources such as books and movies. first idea that will fit both is title:year:length:publisher; where spaces, colons, and Unicode in title are urlescaped+; length is pages or minutes as appropriate; publisher is the printer or production studio.

[1] `https://community.cloudflare.com/t/api-call-suddenly-returns-403-forbidden/396383`

[2] `https://developer.mozilla.org/en-US/docs/Web/API/WebRTC_API/Simple_RTCDataChannel_sample`

Chapter 3

License

GNU GENERAL PUBLIC LICENSE
Version 2, June 1991

Copyright (C) 1989, 1991 Free Software Foundation, Inc.
675 Mass Ave, Cambridge, MA 02139, USA
Everyone is permitted to copy and distribute verbatim copies
of this license document, but changing it is not allowed.

Preamble

The licenses for most software are designed to take away your freedom to share and change it. By contrast, the GNU General Public License is intended to guarantee your freedom to share and change free software--to make sure the software is free for all its users. This General Public License applies to most of the Free Software Foundation's software and to any other program whose authors commit to using it. (Some other Free Software Foundation software is covered by the GNU Library General Public License instead.) You can apply it to your programs, too.

When we speak of free software, we are referring to freedom, not price. Our General Public Licenses are designed to make sure that you have the freedom to distribute copies of free software (and charge for this service if you wish), that you receive source code or can get it if you want it, that you can change the software or use pieces of it in new free programs; and that you know you can do these things.

To protect your rights, we need to make restrictions that forbid anyone to deny you these rights or to ask you to surrender the rights. These restrictions translate to certain responsibilities for you if you distribute copies of the software, or if you modify it.

For example, if you distribute copies of such a program, whether gratis or for a fee, you must give the recipients all the rights that you have. You must make sure that they, too, receive or can get the source code. And you must show them these terms so they know their rights.

We protect your rights with two steps: (1) copyright the software, and (2) offer you this license which gives you legal permission to copy, distribute and/or modify the software.

Also, for each author's protection and ours, we want to make certain that everyone understands that there is no warranty for this free software. If the software is modified by someone else and passed on, we want its recipients to know that what they have is not the original, so that any problems introduced by others will not reflect on the original authors' reputations.

Finally, any free program is threatened constantly by software patents. We wish to avoid the danger that redistributors of a free program will individually obtain patent licenses, in effect making the program proprietary. To prevent this, we have made it clear that any patent must be licensed for everyone's free use or not licensed at all.

The precise terms and conditions for copying, distribution and modification follow.

GNU GENERAL PUBLIC LICENSE
TERMS AND CONDITIONS FOR COPYING, DISTRIBUTION AND MODIFICATION

0. This License applies to any program or other work which contains a notice placed by the copyright holder saying it may be distributed under the terms of this General Public License. The "Program", below, refers to any such program or work, and a "work based on the Program" means either the Program or any derivative work under copyright law: that is to say, a work containing the Program or a portion of it, either verbatim or with modifications and/or translated into another language. (Hereinafter, translation is included without limitation in the term "modification".) Each licensee is addressed as "you".

Activities other than copying, distribution and modification are not covered by this License; they are outside its scope. The act of running the Program is not restricted, and the output from the Program is covered only if its contents constitute a work based on the Program (independent of having been made by running the Program). Whether that is true depends on what the Program does.

1. You may copy and distribute verbatim copies of the Program's source code as you receive it, in any medium, provided that you conspicuously and appropriately publish on each copy an appropriate copyright notice and disclaimer of warranty; keep intact all the notices that refer to this License and to the absence of any warranty; and give any other recipients of the Program a copy of this License along with the Program.

You may charge a fee for the physical act of transferring a copy, and you may at your option offer warranty protection in exchange for a fee.

2. You may modify your copy or copies of the Program or any portion of it, thus forming a work based on the Program, and copy and

distribute such modifications or work under the terms of Section 1 above, provided that you also meet all of these conditions:

a) You must cause the modified files to carry prominent notices stating that you changed the files and the date of any change.

b) You must cause any work that you distribute or publish, that in whole or in part contains or is derived from the Program or any part thereof, to be licensed as a whole at no charge to all third parties under the terms of this License.

c) If the modified program normally reads commands interactively when run, you must cause it, when started running for such interactive use in the most ordinary way, to print or display an announcement including an appropriate copyright notice and a notice that there is no warranty (or else, saying that you provide a warranty) and that users may redistribute the program under these conditions, and telling the user how to view a copy of this License. (Exception: if the Program itself is interactive but does not normally print such an announcement, your work based on the Program is not required to print an announcement.)

These requirements apply to the modified work as a whole. If identifiable sections of that work are not derived from the Program, and can be reasonably considered independent and separate works in themselves, then this License, and its terms, do not apply to those sections when you distribute them as separate works. But when you distribute the same sections as part of a whole which is a work based on the Program, the distribution of the whole must be on the terms of this License, whose permissions for other licensees extend to the entire whole, and thus to each and every part regardless of who wrote it.

Thus, it is not the intent of this section to claim rights or contest your rights to work written entirely by you; rather, the intent is to exercise the right to control the distribution of derivative or collective works based on the Program.

In addition, mere aggregation of another work not based on the Program with the Program (or with a work based on the Program) on a volume of a storage or distribution medium does not bring the other work under the scope of this License.

3. You may copy and distribute the Program (or a work based on it, under Section 2) in object code or executable form under the terms of Sections 1 and 2 above provided that you also do one of the following:

a) Accompany it with the complete corresponding machine-readable source code, which must be distributed under the terms of Sections 1 and 2 above on a medium customarily used for software interchange; or,

b) Accompany it with a written offer, valid for at least three years, to give any third party, for a charge no more than your cost of physically performing source distribution, a complete machine-readable copy of the corresponding source code, to be distributed under the terms of Sections 1 and 2 above on a medium customarily used for software interchange; or,

c) Accompany it with the information you received as to the offer to distribute corresponding source code. (This alternative is allowed only for noncommercial distribution and only if you received the program in object code or executable form with such an offer, in accord with Subsection b above.)

The source code for a work means the preferred form of the work for making modifications to it. For an executable work, complete source code means all the source code for all modules it contains, plus any associated interface definition files, plus the scripts used to control compilation and installation of the executable. However, as a special exception, the source code distributed need not include anything that is normally distributed (in either source or binary form) with the major components (compiler, kernel, and so on) of the operating system on which the executable runs, unless that component itself accompanies the executable.

If distribution of executable or object code is made by offering access to copy from a designated place, then offering equivalent access to copy the source code from the same place counts as distribution of the source code, even though third parties are not compelled to copy the source along with the object code.

4. You may not copy, modify, sublicense, or distribute the Program except as expressly provided under this License. Any attempt otherwise to copy, modify, sublicense or distribute the Program is void, and will automatically terminate your rights under this License. However, parties who have received copies, or rights, from you under this License will not have their licenses terminated so long as such parties remain in full compliance.

5. You are not required to accept this License, since you have not signed it. However, nothing else grants you permission to modify or distribute the Program or its derivative works. These actions are prohibited by law if you do not accept this License. Therefore, by modifying or distributing the Program (or any work based on the Program), you indicate your acceptance of this License to do so, and all its terms and conditions for copying, distributing or modifying the Program or works based on it.

6. Each time you redistribute the Program (or any work based on the Program), the recipient automatically receives a license from the original licensor to copy, distribute or modify the Program subject to these terms and conditions. You may not impose any further restrictions on the recipients' exercise of the rights granted herein. You are not responsible for enforcing compliance by third parties to this License.

7. If, as a consequence of a court judgment or allegation of patent

infringement or for any other reason (not limited to patent issues), conditions are imposed on you (whether by court order, agreement or otherwise) that contradict the conditions of this License, they do not excuse you from the conditions of this License. If you cannot distribute so as to satisfy simultaneously your obligations under this License and any other pertinent obligations, then as a consequence you may not distribute the Program at all. For example, if a patent license would not permit royalty-free redistribution of the Program by all those who receive copies directly or indirectly through you, then the only way you could satisfy both it and this License would be to refrain entirely from distribution of the Program.

If any portion of this section is held invalid or unenforceable under any particular circumstance, the balance of the section is intended to apply and the section as a whole is intended to apply in other circumstances.

It is not the purpose of this section to induce you to infringe any patents or other property right claims or to contest validity of any such claims; this section has the sole purpose of protecting the integrity of the free software distribution system, which is implemented by public license practices. Many people have made generous contributions to the wide range of software distributed through that system in reliance on consistent application of that system; it is up to the author/donor to decide if he or she is willing to distribute software through any other system and a licensee cannot impose that choice.

This section is intended to make thoroughly clear what is believed to be a consequence of the rest of this License.

8. If the distribution and/or use of the Program is restricted in certain countries either by patents or by copyrighted interfaces, the original copyright holder who places the Program under this License may add an explicit geographical distribution limitation excluding those countries, so that distribution is permitted only in or among countries not thus excluded. In such case, this License incorporates the limitation as if written in the body of this License.

9. The Free Software Foundation may publish revised and/or new versions of the General Public License from time to time. Such new versions will be similar in spirit to the present version, but may differ in detail to address new problems or concerns.

Each version is given a distinguishing version number. If the Program specifies a version number of this License which applies to it and "any later version", you have the option of following the terms and conditions either of that version or of any later version published by the Free Software Foundation. If the Program does not specify a version number of this License, you may choose any version ever published by the Free Software Foundation.

10. If you wish to incorporate parts of the Program into other free

programs whose distribution conditions are different, write to the author to ask for permission. For software which is copyrighted by the Free Software Foundation, write to the Free Software Foundation; we sometimes make exceptions for this. Our decision will be guided by the two goals of preserving the free status of all derivatives of our free software and of promoting the sharing and reuse of software generally.

NO WARRANTY

11. BECAUSE THE PROGRAM IS LICENSED FREE OF CHARGE, THERE IS NO WARRANTY FOR THE PROGRAM, TO THE EXTENT PERMITTED BY APPLICABLE LAW. EXCEPT WHEN OTHERWISE STATED IN WRITING THE COPYRIGHT HOLDERS AND/OR OTHER PARTIES PROVIDE THE PROGRAM "AS IS" WITHOUT WARRANTY OF ANY KIND, EITHER EXPRESSED OR IMPLIED, INCLUDING, BUT NOT LIMITED TO, THE IMPLIED WARRANTIES OF MERCHANTABILITY AND FITNESS FOR A PARTICULAR PURPOSE. THE ENTIRE RISK AS TO THE QUALITY AND PERFORMANCE OF THE PROGRAM IS WITH YOU. SHOULD THE PROGRAM PROVE DEFECTIVE, YOU ASSUME THE COST OF ALL NECESSARY SERVICING, REPAIR OR CORRECTION.

12. IN NO EVENT UNLESS REQUIRED BY APPLICABLE LAW OR AGREED TO IN WRITING WILL ANY COPYRIGHT HOLDER, OR ANY OTHER PARTY WHO MAY MODIFY AND/OR REDISTRIBUTE THE PROGRAM AS PERMITTED ABOVE, BE LIABLE TO YOU FOR DAMAGES, INCLUDING ANY GENERAL, SPECIAL, INCIDENTAL OR CONSEQUENTIAL DAMAGES ARISING OUT OF THE USE OR INABILITY TO USE THE PROGRAM (INCLUDING BUT NOT LIMITED TO LOSS OF DATA OR DATA BEING RENDERED INACCURATE OR LOSSES SUSTAINED BY YOU OR THIRD PARTIES OR A FAILURE OF THE PROGRAM TO OPERATE WITH ANY OTHER PROGRAMS), EVEN IF SUCH HOLDER OR OTHER PARTY HAS BEEN ADVISED OF THE POSSIBILITY OF SUCH DAMAGES.

END OF TERMS AND CONDITIONS

Appendix: How to Apply These Terms to Your New Programs

If you develop a new program, and you want it to be of the greatest possible use to the public, the best way to achieve this is to make it free software which everyone can redistribute and change under these terms.

To do so, attach the following notices to the program. It is safest to attach them to the start of each source file to most effectively convey the exclusion of warranty; and each file should have at least the "copyright" line and a pointer to where the full notice is found.

<one line to give the program's name and a brief idea of what it does.>
Copyright (C) 19yy <name of author>

This program is free software; you can redistribute it and/or modify it under the terms of the GNU General Public License as published by the Free Software Foundation; either version 2 of the License, or (at your option) any later version.

This program is distributed in the hope that it will be useful, but WITHOUT ANY WARRANTY; without even the implied warranty of MERCHANTABILITY or FITNESS FOR A PARTICULAR PURPOSE. See the

GNU General Public License for more details.

You should have received a copy of the GNU General Public License
along with this program; if not, write to the Free Software
Foundation, Inc., 675 Mass Ave, Cambridge, MA 02139, USA.

Also add information on how to contact you by electronic and paper mail.

If the program is interactive, make it output a short notice like this when it starts in an interactive mode:

Gnomovision version 69, Copyright (C) 19yy name of author
Gnomovision comes with ABSOLUTELY NO WARRANTY; for details type 'show w'.
This is free software, and you are welcome to redistribute it
under certain conditions; type 'show c' for details.

The hypothetical commands 'show w' and 'show c' should show the appropriate parts of the General Public License. Of course, the commands you use may be called something other than 'show w' and 'show c'; they could even be mouse-clicks or menu items--whatever suits your program.

You should also get your employer (if you work as a programmer) or your school, if any, to sign a "copyright disclaimer" for the program, if necessary. Here is a sample; alter the names:

Yoyodyne, Inc., hereby disclaims all copyright interest in the program
'Gnomovision' (which makes passes at compilers) written by James Hacker.

<signature of Ty Coon>, 1 April 1989
Ty Coon, President of Vice

This General Public License does not permit incorporating your program into proprietary programs. If your program is a subroutine library, you may consider it more useful to permit linking proprietary applications with the library. If this is what you want to do, use the GNU Library General Public License instead of this License.

Chapter 4

Listings

4.1 Root Directory

4.1.1 .gitignore

Listing 4.1: .gitignore

```
*.pyo
*.pyc
*.ico
*.ini
__pycache__
dynamicFiltering.html
Makefile
# allow subdirectory Makefiles to be part of repo
!*/Makefile
kybyz.conf
kybyz.service
kybyz.torrc
python3_plugin.so
pylint3
```

4.1.2 Makefile.template

Listing 4.2: Makefile.template

```
# NOTE: *MUST* change to your own username (also IRC nick) and email address
KB_USERNAME ?= no_more_than_9-chars_is_best
KB_EMAIL ?= 9_char_nick@example.com
APP := kybyz
export

all:
	$(MAKE) -f linux.mk $@
kybyz.%: .FORCE
	$(MAKE) -f linux.mk $@
%:
	$(MAKE) -f linux.mk $@
.FORCE:
	true  # so as to avoid `make -f linux.mk .FORCE`
```

4.1.3 README.md

Listing 4.3: README.md

```
# kybyz
a peer to peer collaboration and social media platform

intended to be a replacement for, among others:

* Facebook
* Twitter/X
* Messenger
* Calendar
* To-do lists

also meant to re-envision, or improve upon:

* [Charles Cameron](https://zenpundit.com/?p=68207)'s hipbone games and
  analysis tools
* curating, and providing human-readable and memorable titles for,
  [IPFS](https://ipfs.tech/) content
* delivery services like DoorDash and <https://w-a-s-t-e.org/>
* rideshare services like Uber and Lyft
* online identity, proof of age, and document signing

if kybyz can incorporate web3 (decentralized finance) functionality, it
will also be able to revolutionize such things as:

* auction sites like ebay
* escrow services
* freelancing sites like Upwork and Toptal

## quickstart

Install and test on a <https://digitalocean.com> Debian-11 droplet,
the cheapest one, currently $6/month.

**NOTE** if these instructions do not work, revert to the same version
as the README. You will be missing the latest functionality, but the
steps have a better chance of working correctly.
I don't test the installation often.

Also: in the following, ‘RH‘ means RedHat-based distros, such as CentOS
and Rocky Linux.


1. Login as root
2. ‘apt update‘  (RH: use ‘yum‘)
3. ‘apt upgrade‘
4. ‘apt install make git xauth‘ (RH: + ‘gcc firefox python3-devel‘)
5. ‘adduser tester‘
6. ‘usermod -a -G sudo tester‘  (will be ‘sudoers‘ on some systems)
7. ‘mkdir ~tester/.ssh‘
9. ‘cp ~/.ssh/authorized_keys ~tester/.ssh/‘
10. ‘chown -R tester.tester ~tester/.ssh‘
```

```

That's all as root; you should now login as a regular user

1. Login as tester; use `ssh -X` to tunnel Xwindows to your local box
2. Set `KB_USERNAME=myusername` and `KB_EMAIL=myemail@example.com`,
   replacing `myusername` and `myemail@example.com` with your own,
   hopefully unique, username and your real email address.
3. ```
   gpg \
     --default-new-key-algo "rsa3072/cert,sign+rsa3072/encr" \
     --pinentry-mode loopback \
     --quick-gen-key "$KB_USERNAME <$KB_EMAIL>" \
       default default never
   ```
   (just hit the enter key at the `Passphrase:` prompt)
4. `mkdir -p src`
5. `cd src`
6. `git clone https://github.com/jcomeauictx/kybyz`
7. `cd kybyz`
8. `cp Makefile.template Makefile`, and edit Makefile with your
   `KB_USERNAME` and `KB_EMAIL` values.
9. `sudo make install && make install` (CS: `sudo make install` will fail
   and you'll need to `make install` separately.)
10. `make` (Wait until the browser launches and you see a cat netmeme.
   There should be a `kbz>` prompt. If not, wait a few seconds and hit the
   enter key, and it should appear.
   If pylint fails, you can still test the app using `make PYLINT=echo
   `
11. Wait for the `kbz>` prompt
12. `send myusername myemail@example.com this is a private message`
   (remember to use your actual kybyz username and email)
13. Watch the log messages and make sure it was sent and received
correctly.
14. Send to another online user. First you'll need to import their public
    GPG key (kybyzdotcom public key is below in this README; copy and
    paste
    it into a plain text file, and name it kybyzdotcom.pub).
15. ^C to get back to the command line.
16. `gpg --import kybyzdotcom.pub`
17. `gpg --sign-key kybyzdotcom`
18. `make`
19. At the `kbz>` prompt: `send kybyzdotcom kybyz@kybyz.com hey this is
Joe`

If kybyzdotcom is online, he'll be able to read your message, but won't
be able to verify who it's from unless he has imported *your* key.

troubleshooting

Testing while chrooting to different debootstrapped systems reveals some
problems. I already mentioned pylint: if the version is too old, it will
complain about many non-problems in the code. For that, just set
PYLINT=echo preceding the `make` command.

```
```

````
If the version of gpg is too old, it will create empty
‘$HOME/.gnupg/secring.gpg‘ and ‘$HOME/.gnupg/pubring.gpg‘ files and break your
current gpg setup. In that case:

 * Remove those two files
 * ‘mkdir -m 0700 $HOME/.gnupg_v1‘
 * Make sure /usr/local/bin precedes /usr/bin in your PATH;
   You can fix this in your ‘$HOME/.bashrc‘ or ‘.bash_aliases‘ files.
 * Create, with mode 755, a file ‘/usr/local/bin/gpg‘ with the following
   contents:
   ‘‘‘bash
   #!/bin/bash
   /usr/bin/gpg --homedir $HOME/.gnupg_v1 "$@"
   ‘‘‘
 * ‘gpg --gen-key‘, and follow the prompts.

If you're helping alpha test, each day before running the script you should
‘git pull‘. This brings in any code changes since the previous attempt.

If you imported the expired kybyzdotcom public key (before 2024-12-29), you
should be able to get the new one using ‘gpg --refresh-keys‘. It seemed to
work automagically for me, anyway. Then when signing with ‘gpg --sign-key‘,
I had to use the entire 40-character ID, instead of "kybyzdotcom", to be
able to sign the new key:
‘gpg --sign-key 341764CDFD52C18832E29A39110861CDBFA29713‘

## proof of authorship

On a platform such as Facebook, proof of authorship is "automatic" in
the sense that, on a centralized platform, everyone has a unique ID
protected by their password. Of course, passwords can be guessed,
phished, or otherwise obtained by other people and thus can impersonate
the author, but generally speaking, if you see a post from jcomeauictx,
you can assume I was the author.

On a peer to peer system it's a lot harder. We'll be using cryptographic
signatures with gpg (GNU's implementation of Pretty Good Privacy, PGP), but
you'll still have to get your public key out to the people you want in your
network using:
 ‘‘‘
 gpg --armor --export me@example.com | \
   mail -s "my public key" myfriend@example.com
 ‘‘‘

## timestamping

In addition to proof of authorship, we will need to have a provable
timestamp, not just the falsifiable "timestamp" field currently in
````

```
example.kybyz/netmeme.json. See
<https://www.jamieweb.net/blog/proof-of-timestamp/> for some ideas on this;
for example, you can embed the hash of the post in a BCH transaction along
with the hash of the previous block. This proves the post is no older than
the previous block, and no newer than the transaction timestamp.

There is now a somewhat-decentralized service for this:
<https://opentimestamps.org/>

## prerequisites

* python3
* gpg

## notes on Android

It can run under Termux. Install from f-droid, not from the App Store.
You will need to install a number of packages, including ‘python‘, ‘uwsgi‘,
and many others I can't think of at the moment. And with ‘pip‘, you will have
to get, at least, ‘pylint‘.

Termux has the uwsgi package, but no plugin for Python, so we must build one.

1. ‘git clone https://github.com/jcomeauictx/uwsgi‘ at the Termux shell
   prompt, and cd to the directory
2. Find what version of uwsgi you have; ‘uwsgi --version‘. I had 2.0.20
3. Check out that version into its own branch:
   ‘git checkout tags/2.0.20 -bv2.0.20‘
4. ‘PYTHON=python3 uwsgi --build-plugin "plugins/python python3"‘
5. ‘cd ../kybyz‘; and ‘ln -s ../uwsgi/python3_plugin.so .‘
6. ‘make‘

## kybyzdotcom public key

‘‘‘
```


```
-----BEGIN PGP PUBLIC KEY BLOCK-----

mQGNBGdxuEQBDADEfYr7yLL8+iedd9rZtJmCZ7k2KJCd3R5CkPTJdD5rhQURh+yp
v5bWkoqLAwWUk1IH7Q2iW5/e8cued/GCBv4Z720JKdhQmq3vs7pxiEZtWc4B79PW
HpQcbYb7ouJXwM16b2GcET2vn9xMaUeVbpePiAr5OiRiLZjDceevzjWyqq/MQlXz
zfct1vbWwlqJml2mvuIsvhuSEpf0zOUqJ6Xlo7unDQ8TtlVEA2YpBSU0IX8tdpal
U1ecVBw5Q9BiDHqepca+w3IwRL9+4zJl3eKvfKLTo8VoMxxyanBizrGQaofBCIGb
qTx0tSGjJggx+5eAs3k/Qxy88f5RSTtk53QODzj1txSe2GWsnahO/t0ABrcAQXgd
t13+ifFQ1F4eli0DtThtwMkhA0OQKmvU7F7BX8BvDbjKatRT3OgwVhCQfGYg9G9t
5+cGvCXPlEwl7J6Yvwze4ysJemYAYjLk+5pxLUpmQK55XjGZgXEQfbbupoWYKXzX
cazQC9CkSZnf+58AEQEAAbQda3lieXpkb3Rjb20gPGt5Ynl6QGt5Ynl6LmNvbT6J
Ac4EEwEKADgWIQQ0F2TN/VLBiDLimjkRCGHNv6KXEwUCZ3G4RAIbAwULCQgHAgYV
CgkICwIEFgIDAQIeAQIXgAAKCRARCGHNv6KXE9zsC/9uiYHfsJFEGSFNTf1l/xKP
0XVhBYgvoGR/1ejsSO0tx34B8SJicGlCBzNvdZc5t06DUs5Uvghosjlje3ZDPeBs
kN5rM755Fe9yBBxxNrqRGuwknzd2vScnrEJ5kMSsZ385myP+USeOVTaiPP8bqXUA
```

```
JnXtYZ2wr0Jx8ctj7MDdYW1bx2wrgX+yfE1j+STBhh0TZhoTDRMblW60IegriRp/
8L5050vJ9b+4tEjYiki8lBIresL/vjNlL1hJLE7Wq3jcwdmpySZz4zJic+nuu0hZ
0lv3oB5zou2GxjN1Bbo7BfT11PZtycMXRbl0kRxx0iWGRNwwPpgVx5DWeuPmVgaa
AHNEjkGPxdn6kSMJDZ99V+wCG5mkBF1+0+nhvHq4B7nGiAkrI9UZpCi0Cq1N82TI
pArytHj0xl1THb6B8/ALCyv0Lt8A0hwSV6eSmaKU0a0B45fTCy7VN59YdMuUzIlK
kbqnkRAA0t8BdnqW+lVu02T9xy4qZU1bvM90Jz87Za65AY0EZ3G4RAEMAL/FAnQM
B0RwAkBA1zZMpXRFxDqUUprxre8P0HE7NAtKSsIujLj+UxX/5Sl3AMEEmG+bD7q2
0JV9lr800+vEWg4rKd4WQF6QYrCc6Ya+408a/aILHAhPqU01JVAVG7a70u5LQahR
mzq4YLVbwpMGBcDGGs0Kfho350wfQCSURVIhg2HsbtPoCIRz1N8q0ljwP3YtTwNX
7rR44hy0oPdukTyM4JnNBa8tNXxuHJ2aycAWSCQ7/2Vm0f0McKWjb6yWIARu6iaY
PE6V63FiQ+7gSE0EWcqD+ITETGhV+o9GZaG2y0Y4f7fB4E1qXqlxGB4R5aYq9xiY
992jS9SH0mBxL4RjLoTia81W6GHi5RQ9mlo8wNtMlnQmItL4FWVZ4g3Wjmfpc0wX
i+8l0ePwiySx8txne/w/JLyxVcK2TiLqqCpZCef+tAndeA00YgK4GWZqqAqf6KfG
LMnnWgk86jfm1CZj+VkyULbiFX/8VnI6whqznYuAAi9+4vFYa1IdBoDB4wARAQAB
iQG2BBgBCgAgFiEENBdkzf1SwYgy4po5EQhhzb+ilxMFAmdxuEQCGwwACgkQEQhh
zb+ilxPhUgwAw8UZZCw7lmLI8jhHMeKwHuVdd6D0/3tgg06C3VSCcxtnLDf1645m
mVtK+Mdaj0I0yrRe5i3yiXuJowVT0JIlDyXc+qg6t8phGVeMv/edJ5Ha56HwQbbK
18DThb9CM2bXMXYnPSMYUI1A103Pz7+IPCP/Zk6wRtRF+UpuKz23180XM3RqvppZ
DIweqyqSl9+5/dTMtdxyvPjmubGEpIDgZ2TlPEg2vhbgts0Cy4Ux22cPY0N0uuYq
yGcqLHinhN9SMdLenLWxqNXwmouDaNk+auD/64BeDR7kgJT0Txz0HgsBoA0c0YRA
W1VwSVtxdsNAZJ0dP29mwnf/Q/SE/VJLj/+Rb8xv90uFD4yZgMJ4IFSv6nx4A0Th
eXTwkj4agFx1a7Gm4raH11hTqU00d0mNSIgVbABtbC9xonSS8opCkivs1FInVJqf
Ct5b/6KeJsXHF2wRKjzBNNej9V8kjjF50QhQcgYTWujgfe8PcH03E9adJYPmjLnb
SnaMYEGiKugA
=LueN
-----END PGP PUBLIC KEY BLOCK-----
```


```
## file storage considerations
using the filesystem as database, at least until I figure out how kybyz
is supposed to work. some random thoughts:

* use file ownership for friends' posts: requires `sudo adduser` to friend
  someone. must add `kybyz` user and group, and add all friends to `kybyz`
  group.
* use `nobody` (add `kybyz` group to it) for not-yet-friended others'
posts.
* subdirectories of `$HOME/.kybyz` for friends, topics, etc.
* file extensions for different types of posts?
* one subdirectory for storage (named `storage`?) for all files,
symlinking
  to other subdirectories as needed?
* split hashes into chunks of 2 or 4 in order to keep inodes per directory
  optimized for fast retrieval? or just use ext4 or xfs and not worry
  about
  it? e.g. `storage/fe/e3/44/2a/fee3442a.txt`

```
developer notes

* Cloudflare, which is used (now, anyway) by ipfs.io, is returning 403
  "Forbidden" [errors on urllib requests](https://community.cloudflare.com
  /t/api-call-suddenly-returns-403-forbidden/396383).
  need to change useragent string. (fixed by commit 6903a329df)
* debugging messages are not shown in console window; the debug log is
```
```

```
  located at `$HOME/.local/log/kybyz.log`
* <https://uwsgi-docs.readthedocs.io/en/latest/WSGIquickstart.html>
* [Heit suggested WebRTC for p2p communication](https://developer.mozilla.org/en-US/docs/Web/API/WebRTC_API/Simple_RTCDataChannel_sample)
* on iphone6 iSH, uwsgi gives error "unable to set PTHREAD_PRIO_INHERIT"
* need to come up with canonical way to list resources such as books and
  movies. first idea that will fit both is title:year:length:publisher;
  where spaces, colons, and Unicode in title are urlescaped+; length is
  pages or minutes as appropriate; publisher is the printer or production
  studio.
```

4.1.4 base58.py

Listing 4.4: base58.py

```
#!/usr/bin/python3
'''
Minimal base58 encoder/decoder

Tried to use https://tools.ietf.org/id/draft-msporny-base58-01.html, but
coding the encoder to the spec gave wrong results, and the decoder instructions
make no sense.

So I ended up using //github.com/jgarzik/python-bitcoinlib/blob/master/
as a basis.

Copyright (C) 2021 jc@unternet.net
'''
import sys, logging  # pylint: disable=multiple-imports
from binascii import unhexlify

BASE58 = b'123456789ABCDEFGHJKLMNPQRSTUVWXYZabcdefghijkmnopqrstuvwxyz'

TEST_VECTORS = [
    # Note that the errors in the draft spec have been corrected below.
    [b'Hello World!', b'2NEpo7TZRRrLZSi2U'],
    [b'Hello, World!', b'72k1xXWG59fYdzSNoA'],
    [b'The quick brown fox jumps over the lazy dog.',
     b'USm3fpXnKG5EUBx2ndxBDMPVciP5hGey2Jh4NDv6gmeo1LkMeiKrLJUUBk6Z'],
    [b'\x00\x00\x00\x28\x7f\xb4\xcd', b'111233QC4'],
    [b'\x00\x00\x28\x7f\xb4\xcd', b'11233QC4'],
]

def encode(bytestring):
    '''
    Base58 encode bytstring
    '''
    cleaned = bytestring.lstrip(b'\0')
    padding = BASE58[0:1] * (len(bytestring) - len(cleaned))
    number, unencoded, encoded = 0, bytearray(bytestring), bytearray()
    while unencoded:
        number = (number << 8) + unencoded.pop(0)
    while number:
        number, remainder = divmod(number, 58)
        encoded.append(BASE58[remainder])
    return (bytes(encoded) + padding)[::-1]

def decode(bytestring):
    '''
    Base58 decode bytestring
    '''
    cleaned = bytestring.lstrip(BASE58[0:1])
    number, decoded = 0, bytearray()
    for byte in cleaned:
        number = (number * 58) + BASE58.index(byte)
```

```
    while number:
        decoded.append(number % 256)
        number >>= 8
    decoded += b'\0' * (len(bytestring) - len(cleaned))
    return bytes(decoded)[::-1]

b58encode, b58decode = encode, decode  # pylint: disable=invalid-name

if __name__ == '__main__':
    logging.basicConfig(level=logging.DEBUG if __debug__ else logging.WARN)
    if len(sys.argv) == 1:
        for DECODED, ENCODED in TEST_VECTORS:
            logging.debug('checking encoding of %r', DECODED)
            check = encode(DECODED)
            if check != ENCODED:
                logging.error('%r does not match %r', check, ENCODED)
        for DECODED, ENCODED in TEST_VECTORS:
            logging.debug('checking decoding of %r', ENCODED)
            check = decode(ENCODED)
            if check != DECODED:
                logging.error('%r does not match %r', check, DECODED)
    elif sys.argv[1] == 'encode':
        if sys.argv[2:]:
            # assume hexlified binary data
            INBYTES = unhexlify(''.join(sys.argv[2:]))
        else:
            # assume raw binary data
            INBYTES = sys.stdin.buffer.read()
        sys.stdout.buffer.write(encode(INBYTES))
    elif sys.argv[1] == 'decode':
        # assume base58-encoded data from either commandline or stdin
        if sys.argv[2:]:
            INBYTES = ''.join(sys.argv[2:]).encode()
        else:
            INBYTES = sys.stdin.buffer.read().rstrip()
        sys.stdout.buffer.write(decode(INBYTES))
    else:
        raise ValueError('Only accepted args: "encode" or "decode"')
```

4.1.5 canonical_json.py

Listing 4.5: canonical_json.py

```
#!/usr/bin/python3
'''
kybyz version 0.1, since original has foundered

this will be built on ipfs, using canonical json objects
'''
import sys, json, logging  # pylint: disable=multiple-imports

def canonicalize(obj):
    '''
    dump object as canonical json

    https://gibson042.github.io/canonicaljson-spec/ and
    http://wiki.laptop.org/go/Canonical_JSON for reference

    if it's not json, just return it as is.

    >>> print(canonicalize({'test': [1, 2, 3, 'test again']}), end='')
    {"test":[1,2,3,"test again"]}
    '''
    if isinstance(obj, str):
        logging.debug('object passed as string: %s', obj)
        try:
            obj = json.loads(obj)
        except ValueError:
            logging.debug('%r does not represent a valid Python object', obj)
            return obj
    logging.debug('object being canonicalized: %s', obj)
    result = json.dumps(
        obj,
        ensure_ascii=False,  # is this correct by the standard?
        separators=(',', ':'),  # no unnecessary whitespace
        sort_keys=True,
    )
    return result

if __name__ == '__main__':
    logging.basicConfig(level=logging.DEBUG if __debug__ else logging.INFO)
    try:
        print(canonicalize(sys.argv[1]), end='')  # no trailing whitespace
    except IndexError:
        print('Must pass a single string representing JSON object')
```

4.1.6 ircbot.py

Listing 4.6: ircbot.py

```
#!/usr/bin/python3
'''
IRC communications for server discovery
'''
# pylint: disable=multiple-imports
# the following is for newer, pip-installed pylint
# pylint: disable=bad-option-value, consider-using-f-string
import sys, os, socket, pwd, threading, time
from kbcommon import CACHED, logging, TO_PAGE, CHANNEL, JSON, POSTS_QUEUE
from kbutils import decrypt, check_username

IRCSERVER = 'irc.lfnet.org'
PORT = 6667
BUFFERSIZE = 16 * 1024  # make it big enough to get full banner from IRC server
CRLF = '\r\n'
TIMEOUT = int(os.getenv('KB_DELAY') or 600)
MAXSIZE = 1024 * 1024
MAXCACHE = MAXSIZE * 1024

class IRCBot():
    '''
    Implements IRC client

    see https://www.techbeamers.com/create-python-irc-bot/
    also https://datatracker.ietf.org/doc/html/rfc2812
    '''
    # pylint: disable=too-many-instance-attributes
    def __init__(self, server=IRCSERVER, port=PORT,
                 nickname=None, realname=None):
        '''
        initialize the client
        '''
        self.client = self.stream = None  # set by connect()
        self.server = server
        self.port = port
        self.nickname = nickname or pwd.getpwuid(os.geteuid()).pw_name
        # NOTE: when we implement true p2p networking, realname should include
        # connection port (or maybe not, now that we're using KB_COMMS)
        self.realname = realname or pwd.getpwuid(os.geteuid()).pw_gecos
        self.connect(server, port, self.nickname, self.realname)
        self.terminate = False
        daemon = threading.Thread(target=self.monitor, name='ircbot_daemon')
        daemon.daemon = True
        daemon.start()

    def nick(self, nickname):
        '''
        set new nickname
```

```
        '''
        self.client.send(('NICK %s\r\n' % nickname).encode())

    def join(self, channel=CHANNEL):
        '''
        join a new channel
        '''
        self.client.send(('JOIN %s\r\n' % channel).encode())

    def leave(self, channel=CHANNEL):
        '''
        join a new channel
        '''
        self.client.send(('PART %s\r\n' % channel).encode())

    def user(self, nickname, realname):
        '''
        tell server the names (the tuple (nickname, realname)) to use
        '''
        names = (nickname, realname)
        self.client.send(('USER %s 0 * :%s\r\n' % names).encode())

    def connect(self, server, port, nickname, realname):
        '''
        connect to the server and identify ourselves
        '''
        self.client = socket.socket(socket.AF_INET, socket.SOCK_STREAM)
        # enable keepalives at the socket (SOL_SOCKET) level
        self.client.setsockopt(socket.SOL_SOCKET, socket.SO_KEEPALIVE, 1)
        # after 1 second of TCP inactivity, trigger keepalive pings
        self.client.setsockopt(socket.IPPROTO_TCP, socket.TCP_KEEPIDLE, 1)
        # send a keepalive ping every 60 seconds
        self.client.setsockopt(socket.IPPROTO_TCP, socket.TCP_KEEPINTVL, 60)
        # quit after 5 consecutive failures
        self.client.setsockopt(socket.IPPROTO_TCP, socket.TCP_KEEPCNT, 5)
        self.stream = self.client.makefile()
        self.client.connect((server, port))
        self.user(nickname, realname)
        self.nick(nickname)
        self.join(CHANNEL)

    def privmsg(self, target, message):
        '''
        simulates typing a message in ircII with no preceding command

        target should be a channel name preceded by '#', or nick

        message should not have any embedded CRLFs, or non-ASCII characters.
        '''
        sep = '\xa0'  # separates prefix from message
        logging.debug('message: %r', message)
```

```
        testmsg = ' '.join([CACHED['irc_id'], 'PRIVMSG', target, sep + message])
        logging.debug('testmsg: %s', testmsg.replace(sep, ':'))
        if len(testmsg) <= 510:
            self.sendchunk(('PRIVMSG %s :%s\r\n' % (target, message)).encode())
        else:
            pieces = testmsg[:510].split(sep)
            chunklength = len(pieces[-1])
            for chunk in [message[i:i+chunklength]
                          for i in range(0, len(message), chunklength)]:
                logging.debug('sending chunk %s', chunk)
                self.sendchunk(
                    ('PRIVMSG %s %s\r\n' % (target, chunk)).encode())

    def sendchunk(self, chunk):
        '''
        send a chunk. it must already be UTF8 encoded
        '''
        sent, tries = False, 0
        while not sent:
            try:
                self.client.send(chunk)
                sent = True
                tries = 0 # only abandon after several *consecutive* tries
            except BrokenPipeError:
                logging.debug('lost connection, waiting for monitor to rejoin')
                tries += 1
                if tries == 5:
                    raise
                time.sleep(3)

    def monitor(self):
        '''
        wait for input. send a PONG for every PING

        intended to run in a daemon thread

        set ircbot.terminate to True in order to shut it down
        '''
        logging.debug('ircbot monitoring incoming traffic')
        tries = 0
        while tries < 10:
            try:
                received = self.stream.readline().rstrip()
                tries = 0
            except ConnectionResetError:
                tries += 1
                self.connect(self.server, self.port,
                             self.nickname, self.realname)
                continue
```

```
            logging.info('received: %r, length: %d', received, len(received))
            end_message = len(received) < 510
            # make sure all words[n] references are accounted for
            words = received.split() + ['', '', '']
            nickname, matched = check_username(words[0])
            if words[0] == 'PING':
                pong = received.replace('I', 'O', 1).rstrip() + CRLF
                logging.info('sending: %r', pong)
                self.client.send(pong.encode())
            elif words[1] == 'JOIN' and matched:
                CACHED['irc_id'] = words[0]
                logging.info("CACHED['irc_id'] = %s", CACHED['irc_id'])
            elif words[1] == 'PRIVMSG':
                sender = nickname
                privacy = 'public' if words[2] == CHANNEL else 'private'
                logging.info('%s message received from %s:', privacy, sender)
                # chop preceding ':' from ':this is a private message'
                CACHED[sender] += ' '.join(words[3:])[1:].rstrip()
                # try decoding what we have so far
                # gnupg will log a warning if unsuccessful
                logging.debug('attempting to decode %s', CACHED[sender])
                text, trustlevel = decrypt(CACHED[sender].encode())
                logging.debug('text: %s, trustlevel: %s', text, trustlevel)
                if text or end_message:
                    text = text or CACHED[sender][:256].encode()
                    logging.info('(ignore any warnings above from gnupg; '
                                 'the message, once complete, was '
                                 'successfully decrypted)')
                    logging.info(
                        '%s %s message from %s: %s',
                        trustlevel,
                        privacy,
                        sender,
                        text.decode().replace('<', '&lt;').replace('>', '&gt;'),
                        **TO_PAGE)
                    if JSON.match(CACHED[sender]):
                        POSTS_QUEUE.append(CACHED[sender])
                        logging.debug('appended %r to POSTS_QUEUE',
                                      CACHED[sender])
                    else:
                        logging.debug('Not JSON: %s', CACHED[sender])
                    CACHED[sender] = ''
                elif len(CACHED[sender]) > MAXSIZE:
                    logging.info(
                        'clearing overflow CACHED[%s]: %r..., length %d',
                        sender, CACHED[sender][:256], len(CACHED[sender]))
                    CACHED[sender] = ''
                else:
                    logging.debug('CACHED[%s] now %r', sender, CACHED[sender])
```

```
            clearcache()
        logging.warning('ircbot terminated from launching thread')

def test(nickname=None, realname=None):
    '''
    run a bot from the command line, for testing
    '''
    ircbot = type('IRCBot', (), {'terminate': False})()
    try:
        ircbot = IRCBot(nickname=nickname, realname=realname)
        time.sleep(TIMEOUT)
    except KeyboardInterrupt:
        logging.warning('Telling monitor to terminate')
        ircbot.terminate = True

def clearcache(maxcache=MAXCACHE):
    '''
    delete entries if CACHED size is greater than MAXCACHE

    >>> CACHED.update({':2': 'x' * 1024, ':1': 'y' * 64, ':3': 'z' * 2048})
    >>> logging.debug('sum of lengths: %d', sum(map(len,
    ...  [v for k, v in CACHED.items() if k.startswith(':')])))
    >>> logging.info('doctest CACHED.keys(): %s', list(CACHED.keys()))
    >>> clearcache(100)
    >>> {k: v for k, v in CACHED.items() if k.startswith(':')}
    {':1': 'yyyyyyyyyyyyyyyyyyyyyyyyyyyyyyyyyyyyyyyyyyyyyyyyyyyyyyyyyyyyyyyy'}
    >>> len(CACHED[':1'])
    64
    '''
    logging.debug('CACHED.keys(): %s', list(CACHED.keys()))
    while sum(map(len, [v for k, v in CACHED.items()
                        if k.startswith(':')])) > maxcache:
        next_biggest = max({k: v for k, v in CACHED.items()
                            if k.startswith(':')},
                           key=lambda k: len(CACHED[k]))
        logging.debug('next_biggest: %s', next_biggest)
        logging.warning('deleting CACHED[%s] of length %d', next_biggest,
                        len(CACHED[next_biggest]))
        del CACHED[next_biggest]

if __name__ == '__main__':
    sys.argv.extend(['', ''])  # in case no args given
    test(nickname=sys.argv[1], realname=sys.argv[2])
```

4.1.7 kbcommon.py

Listing 4.7: kbcommon.py

```
#!/usr/bin/python3
'''
common data structures needed by various parts of kybyz
'''
import sys, os, logging, re  # pylint: disable=multiple-imports
from collections import defaultdict, deque, namedtuple
from datetime import datetime, timezone

COMMAND = os.path.splitext(os.path.basename(sys.argv[0]))[0]
ARGS = sys.argv[1:]
EXAMPLE = 'example.kybyz'  # subdirectory with sample posts
CACHED = defaultdict(str, {'uptime': None})
HOME = os.path.expanduser('~')
CACHE = os.path.join(HOME, '.kybyz')
KYBYZ_HOME = os.path.join(CACHE, 'home')
BASE_LOG_FORMAT = '%(levelname)s:%(name)s:%(message)s'
EXTENDED_LOG_FORMAT = '%(asctime)s:%(threadName)s:' + BASE_LOG_FORMAT
LOG_TIMESTAMP_FORMAT = '%Y-%m-%d %H:%M:%S'
LOGDIR = os.getenv('KB_LOGDIR', os.path.join(HOME, 'log'))
os.makedirs(LOGDIR, exist_ok=True)
LOGFILE = os.path.join(os.path.join(LOGDIR, 'kybyz.log'))
LOGSTREAM_HANDLER = logging.StreamHandler()
# limit logging to screen when using kbz> commandline
LOGLEVEL = logging.DEBUG if ARGS or os.getenv('KB_DEBUG') else logging.INFO
if not os.path.split(sys.argv[0])[1].endswith(('doctest', 'doctest.py')):
    LOGSTREAM_HANDLER.setLevel(LOGLEVEL)
LOGFILE_HANDLER = logging.FileHandler(LOGFILE)
LOGFILE_HANDLER.setLevel(logging.DEBUG)
LOGFILE_HANDLER.setFormatter(logging.Formatter(EXTENDED_LOG_FORMAT))
MESSAGE_QUEUE = deque(maxlen=1024)
POSTS_QUEUE = deque(maxlen=1024)
TO_PAGE = {'extra': {'to_page': True}}
REGISTRATION = namedtuple('registration', ('username', 'email', 'gpgkey'))
CHANNEL = '#kybyz'
JSON = re.compile(r'^\{.*\}$')

class DequeHandler(logging.NullHandler):
    '''
    simple handler to append log record to queue

    >>> logging.debug('test')
    >>> logging.debug('test to page', **TO_PAGE)
    '''
    def handle(self, record):
        if hasattr(record, 'to_page') and record.to_page:
            #logging.debug('adding to MESSAGE_QUEUE: %s', record)
            MESSAGE_QUEUE.append(':'.join([
                record.name,
                record.levelname,
                record.msg % record.args
```

```
            ]))

LOGQUEUE_HANDLER = DequeHandler()
LOGQUEUE_HANDLER.setLevel(logging.INFO)

logging.basicConfig(
    level=logging.DEBUG if __debug__ else logging.INFO,
    format=BASE_LOG_FORMAT,
    handlers=[LOGSTREAM_HANDLER, LOGFILE_HANDLER, LOGQUEUE_HANDLER]
)
logging.info('COMMAND: %s, ARGS: %s', COMMAND, ARGS)

def read(filename):
    '''
    read and return file contents
    '''
    with open(filename, 'rb') as infile:
        return infile.read()

def make_timestamp():
    '''
    untrusted timestamp.

    will need blockchain for a trusted timestamp
    '''
    return datetime.now(timezone.utc).isoformat()

def tuplify(versionstring):
    '''
    convert version string to tuple of integers

    >>> tuplify('0.0.1')
    (0, 0, 1)
    >>> max(['0.0.100', '0.0.11'])
    '0.0.11'
    >>> max(['0.0.100', '0.0.11'], key=tuplify)
    '0.0.100'
    '''
    return tuple(int(s) for s in versionstring.split('.'))

# pylint: disable=unused-argument
if COMMAND == 'doctest':
    def doctestdebug(message, *args, **kwargs):
        '''
        show debugging message only during doctests
        '''
        logging.debug(message, *args, **kwargs)
else:
    def doctestdebug(message, *args, **kwargs):
        '''
        debugging message not shown outside of doctests
        '''
        pass  # pylint: disable=unnecessary-pass
# vim: tabstop=8 expandtab shiftwidth=4 softtabstop=4
```

4.1.8 kbgpg.py

Listing 4.8: kbgpg.py

```
#!/usr/bin/python3
'''
made for developing without functional python-gnupg package

this is probably not needed. I didn't realize that `gnupg` and `python-gnupg`
were two separate PyPI (pip) packages until Ildar told me -- jc
'''
import subprocess, re  # pylint: disable=multiple-imports
from kbcommon import logging

logging.warning('Using primitive GPG functionality')

def run_process(command, **kwargs):
    '''
    implementation of subprocess.run for older Python3

    https://pymotw.com/3/subprocess/
    '''
    text_input = kwargs.get('input', None)
    capture_output = kwargs.get('capture_output', False)
    logging.debug('capture_output %s ignored', capture_output)
    timeout = kwargs.get('timeout', None)
    check = kwargs.get('check', None)
    if timeout:
        raise NotImplementedError('"timeout" not supported')
    # pylint: disable=bad-option-value, consider-using-with
    process = subprocess.Popen(
        command,
        stdin=kwargs.get('stdin', subprocess.PIPE),
        stdout=kwargs.get('stdout', subprocess.PIPE),
        stderr=kwargs.get('stderr', subprocess.PIPE),
        # pylint: disable=bad-option-value, consider-using-dict-items
        **{k: kwargs[k] for k in kwargs if k not in
           ['input', 'capture_output', 'timeout', 'check']}
    )
    stdout, stderr = process.communicate(text_input)
    if check and process.returncode:
        raise subprocess.CalledProcessError(process.returncode, command,
                                            output=(stdout, stderr))
    return type('', (), {
        'stdout': stdout,
        'stderr': stderr,
    })

class GPG():
    '''
    drop-in replacement for python3-gnupg class

    limited to the few calls that kybyz makes,
    and only for English language, among other limitations.
```

```
    '''
    def __init__(self, options=None):
        '''
        add subprocess.run replacement if it doesn't exist
        '''
        if not hasattr(subprocess, 'run'):
            subprocess.run = run_process
        else:
            try:
                subprocess.run(['ls'], capture_output=True, check=True)
            except TypeError:  # Python3.5
                subprocess.run = run_process
        options = options or []
        self.defaultkey = None
        if len(options) >= 2 and options[0] == '--default-key':
            self.defaultkey = options[1]

    def sign(self, data, keyid=None):
        '''
        gpg sign given data

        unlike python-gnupg, return as binary data

        NOTE: side effect: sets self.defaultkey if not set by constructor
        '''
        self.defaultkey = self.defaultkey or keyid
        command = ['gpg', '--sign']
        if self.defaultkey:
            command.extend(['--default-key', self.defaultkey])
        run = subprocess.run(
            command,
            input=data,
            capture_output=True,
            check=True)
        run.data = run.stdout
        return run

    def encrypt(self, data, recipients, **kwargs):
        '''
        gpg encrypt data for recipients
        '''
        self.defaultkey = self.defaultkey or kwargs.get('keyid', None)
        command = ['gpg', '--encrypt']
        if self.defaultkey:
            command.extend(['--defaultkey', self.defaultkey])
        for recipient in recipients:
            command.extend(['-r', recipient])
        if kwargs.get('sign', None):
            command.append('--sign')
        if kwargs.get('armor', None):
            command.append('--armor')
        run = subprocess.run(command, input=data,
                             capture_output=True, check=False)
        run.data = run.stdout
```

```
        return run

    def decrypt(self, data, keyid=None):
        '''
        gpg decrypt data
        '''
        self.defaultkey = self.defaultkey or keyid
        command = ['gpg', '--decrypt']
        if self.defaultkey:
            command.extend(['--default-key', self.defaultkey])
        run = subprocess.run(
            command,
            input=data,
            capture_output=True,
            check=False)
        run.data = run.stdout
        logging.debug('decrypt stderr: %s', run.stderr)
        output = list(filter(None, run.stderr.decode().split('\n')))
        logging.debug('looking for username and trust_text in %s',
                      output[-1])
        try:
            run.username, run.trust_text = re.compile(
                r'^gpg: Good signature from "([^"]+)" \[([^]]+)\]$').match(
                    output[-1]).groups()
        except AttributeError:
            run.username = run.trust_text = None
        return run

    def verify(self, signed):
        '''
        verify signature on given signed data
        '''
        run = subprocess.run(['gpg', '--verify'], input=signed,
                             capture_output=True, check=False)
        output = run.stderr.decode().split('\n')
        combined = ' '.join(output)
        try:
            run.timestamp = re.compile(
                r'^gpg: Signature made (.*?)(?: using .*)?$').match(
                    output[0]).groups()[0]
            # NOTE: 'self' added to following log simply to defeat
            # recent 'no-self-use' addition to pylint
            logging.debug('%s: run.timestamp: %s', self, run.timestamp)
            run.key_id = re.compile(
                r' using RSA key (?:ID )?([0-9A-F]{8,40})\s').search(
                    combined).groups()[0]
            logging.debug('run.key_id: %s', run.key_id)
            pattern = re.compile(
                r' Good signature from "([^"]+)"(?: \[([^]]+)\])?')
            logging.debug('pattern: %s', pattern)
            run.username, run.trust_text = pattern.search(combined).groups()
            logging.debug('run.username: %s, run.trust_text: %s',
```

```
                            run.username, run.trust_text)
        except (AttributeError, IndexError) as problem:
            logging.exception('did not find needed data in %r', combined)
            raise problem
        return run
```

4.1.9 kbutils.py

Listing 4.9: kbutils.py

```
#!/usr/bin/python3
'''
Kybyz utilities
'''
# pylint: disable=bad-option-value, consider-using-f-string
import os, re, subprocess, json  # pylint: disable=multiple-imports
from hashlib import sha256
from base58 import b58encode, b58decode
from canonical_json import canonicalize
from kbcommon import CACHE, CACHED, EXAMPLE, KYBYZ_HOME, COMMAND, ARGS, logging
from kbcommon import REGISTRATION, read, CHANNEL, POSTS_QUEUE, JSON
from post import BasePost

try:
    from gnupg import GPG
except ImportError:
    from kbgpg import GPG

def kbhash(message):
    '''
    return base58 of sha256 hash of message, with prefix 'kbz'

    >>> kbhash({'test': 0})
    'kbz6cd8vvJh7zja18Nju1GTuCNKqhDdFo7RCWvVbjHyqEuv'
    '''
    prefix = b'\x07\x88\xcc'  # when added to 32-byte string produces 'kbz'
    canonical = canonicalize(message).encode()
    hashed = sha256(canonical).digest()
    return b58encode(prefix + hashed).decode()

def verify_key(email):
    '''
    fetch user's GPG key and make sure it matches given email address
    '''
    gpgkey = None
    gpg = GPG()
    # pylint: disable=no-member
    verified = gpg.verify(gpg.sign('', keyid=email).data)
    logging.debug('verified: %s', verified)
    if not verified.username.endswith('<' + email + '>'):
        raise ValueError('%s no match for GPG certificate %s' %
                         (email, verified.username))
    gpgkey = verified.key_id
    return gpgkey

def publish(post_id, publish_to='all'):
    '''
    send post out to network

```

```
    unencrypted if to='all', otherwise encrypted to each recipient with
    their own keys
    '''
    posts = find_posts(KYBYZ_HOME, post_id)
    post_count = len(posts)
    if post_count != 1:
        raise ValueError('No posts matching %r' % post_id if post_count == 0
                         else 'Ambiguous suffix %r matches %s' % (
                             posts))
    recipients = publish_to.split(',')
    for recipient in recipients:
        logging.debug('recipient: %s', recipient)
        if recipient == 'all':
            send(CHANNEL, '-', read(posts[0]))
        else:
            send(recipient, recipient, read(posts[0]))

def send(recipient, email, *words):
    '''
    encrypt, sign, and send a private message to recipient

    `recipient` is the 'nick' (nickname) of the user to whom you wish to send
    the message. `email` is not necessarily an email address, but is used to
    find the GPG key of the recipient.

    use `-` instead of email to send plain text
    '''
    if len(words) > 1 or isinstance(words[0], str):
        text = ' '.join(words).encode()
    else:
        text = words[0]  # as when called by `publish`
    logging.debug('words: %s', words)
    encoded = None
    if email != '-':
        user = "%s <%s>" % (recipient, email)
        gpg = GPG()
        logging.debug('message before encrypting: %s', text)
        encrypted = gpg.encrypt(
            text,  # pylint: disable=no-member
            [user],
            sign=True,
            armor=False)
        logging.debug('encrypted: %r...', encrypted.data[:64])
        encoded = b58encode(encrypted.data).decode()
        logging.debug('encoded: %s', encoded)
    if text and not encoded:
        if email == '-' or os.getenv('KB_SEND_PLAINTEXT_OK'):
            logging.warning('encryption %s, sending plaintext',
                            'bypassed' if email == '-' else 'failed')
            encoded = text.decode()
        else:
```

```
            logging.warning('encryption failed, run with '
                            'KB_SEND_PLAINTEXT_OK=1 to send anyway')
            logging.warning('setting message to "(encryption failed)"')
            encoded = '(encryption failed)'
    CACHED['ircbot'].privmsg(recipient, encoded)

def registration():
    '''
    get and return information on user, if any

    assume only one key for user's email address, for now.
    we should probably pick the one with the latest expiration date.
    '''
    username = email = gpgkey = None
    links = []
    if os.path.exists(KYBYZ_HOME):
        try:
            links.append(os.readlink(KYBYZ_HOME))
            username = os.path.basename(links[-1])
            links.append(os.readlink(links[-1]))
            email = os.path.basename(links[-1])
            links.append(os.readlink(links[-1]))
            gpgkey = os.path.basename(links[-1])
            logging.debug('links found: %s', links)
        except OSError:
            logging.exception('Bad registration at %s', links[-1])
    return REGISTRATION(username, email, gpgkey)

def register(username=None, email=None, gpgkey=None):
    '''
    register kybyz account
    '''
    if gpgkey is None:
        gpgkey = verify_key(email)
    current = registration()  # see what we already have, if anything
    if username is None or email is None:
        logging.error('Usage: %s %s USERNAME EMAIL_ADDRESS',
                      COMMAND, ARGS[0])
        raise ValueError('Must specify desired username and email address')
    if any(current):
        if (username, email, gpgkey) != current:
            raise ValueError('Previously registered as %s %s %s' % current)
        logging.warning('Already registered as %s %s %s', *current)
    else:
        os.makedirs(os.path.join(CACHE, gpgkey))
        os.symlink(os.path.join(CACHE, gpgkey), os.path.join(CACHE, email))
        os.symlink(os.path.join(CACHE, email), os.path.join(CACHE, username))
        os.symlink(os.path.join(CACHE, username), KYBYZ_HOME)
        logging.info('Now registered as %s %s %s', username, email, gpgkey)
```

```
        if CACHED.get('ircbot', None):
            CACHED['ircbot'].nick(username)
            CACHED['ircbot'].leave()  # rejoin to freshen CACHED['irc_id']
            CACHED['ircbot'].join()
        else:
            logging.info('registering outside of running application')

def create(post_type, *args, returned='hashed', **kwargs):
    '''
    make a new post from the command line or from another subroutine
    '''
    if len(args) == 1 and JSON.match(args[0]):
        try:
            kwargs.update(json.loads(args[0]))
        except json.decoder.JSONDecodeError:
            logging.error('Post not valid JSON format: %s' % args[0])
    else:
        logging.debug('args %s not valid JSON, using as key-value pairs', args)
        for arg in args:
            logging.debug('parsing %s', arg)
            try:
                kwargs.update(dict((arg.split('=', 1),)))
            except ValueError:
                logging.warning('ignoring poorly formatted key-value pair %r',
                                arg
                )
    # override post_type if specified
    if post_type:
        kwargs.update({'type': post_type})
    try:
        newpost = BasePost(None, **kwargs)
        jsonified = newpost.to_json()
        post_type = newpost.type
        hashed = kbhash(jsonified)
        cached = cachewrite('.'.join((hashed, post_type)), jsonified)
        # make another, canonicalized, copy for a unique hash
        jsonified = newpost.to_json(for_hashing=True)
        hashed = kbhash(jsonified)
        hashcached = cachewrite('.'.join((hashed, post_type)), jsonified)
        unadorned = os.path.splitext(hashcached)[0]
        try:
            os.symlink(cached, unadorned)
        except FileExistsError:
            existing = os.readlink(unadorned)
            if existing != cached:
                logging.warning('updating post %s to %s', unadorned, cached)
                os.unlink(unadorned)
                os.symlink(cached, unadorned)
            else:
                logging.debug('%s already symlinked to %s', unadorned, cached)
```

```
        return hashed if returned == 'hashed' else newpost
    except AttributeError:
        logging.exception('Post failed: attribute error')
        return None
    except TypeError:
        logging.exception('Post failed with kwargs: %s', kwargs)
        return None

def cachewrite(path, data):
    '''
    store data in cache for later retrieval
    '''
    fullpath = os.path.realpath(os.path.join(KYBYZ_HOME, path))
    if not fullpath.startswith(os.path.realpath(KYBYZ_HOME) + os.sep):
        raise ValueError('Attempt to write %s outside of app bounds' %
        fullpath)
    os.makedirs(os.path.dirname(fullpath), exist_ok=True)
    binary = 'b' if isinstance(data, bytes) else ''
    try:
        with open(fullpath, 'x' + binary) as outfile:
            outfile.write(data)
    except FileExistsError:
        existing = read(fullpath)
        if data != existing:
            logging.error('Failed to update %s from %r to %r', fullpath,
                          existing, data)
        else:
            logging.debug('% already cached', fullpath)
    return fullpath

def guess_mimetype(filename, contents):
    '''
    guess and return mimetype based on name and/or contents
    '''
    logging.debug('filename: %s, contents: %r', filename, contents[:32])
    extension = os.path.splitext(filename)[1]
    mimetypes = {
        '.jpg': 'image/jpeg',
        '.css': 'text/css',
    }
    return mimetypes.get(extension, 'text/html')

def get_posts(directory, pattern=None, convert=None):
    '''
    get list of posts

    we use only those symlinked to by unadorned hashes
    '''
    pattern = re.compile(pattern or '^kbz[0-9A-Za-z]*$')
    filenames = [os.path.join(directory, filename)
                 for filename in os.listdir(directory)
                 if pattern.match(filename)]
    convert = convert or str  # or specify convert=os.path.realpath
    return [convert(filename) for filename in filenames
```

```
            if os.path.islink(filename)]

def find_posts(directory, suffix):
    '''
    get list of posts matching suffix
    '''
    posts = get_posts(directory, '^kbz[0-9A-Za-z]*%s$' % suffix)
    return posts

def loadposts(to_html=True, tries=0):
    '''
    fetch and return all posts from KYBYZ_HOME or, if empty, from EXAMPLE

    setting to_html to True forces conversion from JSON format to HTML
    '''
    logging.debug('running loadposts(%s)', to_html)
    if not get_posts(KYBYZ_HOME):
        if tries > 1:
            raise ValueError('No posts found after example posts cached')
        # populate KYBYZ_HOME from EXAMPLE
        for example in get_posts(EXAMPLE):
            create(None, read(example).decode())
        return loadposts(to_html, tries=tries + 1)
    # now cache any that came in over the wire
    for index in range(len(POSTS_QUEUE)):  # pylint: disable=unused-variable
        create(None, POSTS_QUEUE.popleft())
    get_post = BasePost if to_html else read
    posts = [get_post(p) for p in get_posts(KYBYZ_HOME)]
    return sorted(filter(None, posts), key=lambda p: p.timestamp, reverse=True)

def ipfs_add(filepath):
    '''
    add a file to IPFS
    '''
    exitcode, output = subprocess.getstatusoutput(['ipfs', 'add', filepath])
    if exitcode != 0:
        logging.error('adding "%s" to IPFS failed with code %d',
                      filepath, exitcode)
        return None
    words = output.split()
    return words[1]

def decrypt(message):
    '''
    decrypt a message sent to me, and verify sender email
    '''
    gpg = GPG()
    verified = decoded = b''
    logging.debug('decoding %s...', message[:64])
    try:
        decoded = b58decode(message)
```

```
        logging.debug('decrypting %r...', decoded[:64])
        decrypted = gpg.decrypt(decoded)
        # pylint: disable=no-member
        verified = 'trust level %s' % decrypted.trust_text
    except ValueError:
        logging.warning('%r... not base58 encoded', message[:32])
        decrypted = type('', (), {'data': message})
        verified = 'unencoded'
    except subprocess.CalledProcessError as problem:
        logging.exception(problem)
        decrypted = type('', (), {'data': b''})
    return decrypted.data, verified

def check_username(identifier):
    '''
    identifier is :bleah!bleah@bleah.com' and CACHED['username'] == 'bleah'

    >>> CACHED['username'] = 'bleah'
    >>> check_username(':bleah!bleah@bleah.com')
    ('bleah', True)
    >>> check_username(':blah!bleah@bleah.com')
    ('blah', False)
    >>> check_username(':irc.lfnet.org')
    (None, None)
    '''
    try:
        start = identifier.index(':') + 1
        end = identifier.index('!')
        nickname = identifier[start:end]
        logging.debug('identifier: %s, start: %s, end: %s, check: %s',
                      identifier, start, end, nickname)
        matched = CACHED.get('username', None) == nickname
    except ValueError:
        # ignore failure, because PINGs don't have username anyway
        #logging.error('cannot find nickname in %s', identifier)
        nickname = matched = None
    return nickname, matched
# vim: tabstop=8 expandtab shiftwidth=4 softtabstop=4
```

4.1.10 kybyz.css

Listing 4.10: kybyz.css

```
.icon {
  margin: auto;
  width: 1em;
  height: 1em;
  text-align: center;
}
```

4.1.11 kybyz.html

Listing 4.11: kybyz.html

```
<div class="kybyz">
  <span class="icon" title="{post.text}">{post.text}</span>
</div>
```

4.1.12 kybyz.ini

Listing 4.12: kybyz.ini

```
[uwsgi]
http-socket = kybyz:$(KB_WEB)
socket = $(TMPDIR)/kybyz.sock
enable-threads
plugin = python3
wsgi-file = kybyz.py
callable = serve
need-app = true
honour-stdin
disable-logging
pidfile2 = $(TMPDIR)/kybyz.pid
```

4.1.13 kybyz.js

Listing 4.13: kybyz.js

```
if (typeof(com) == "undefined") com = {};
com.kybyz = {};
com.kybyz.app = {};
com.kybyz.app.UpdateInterval = 1000;  // milliseconds, start off slow
com.kybyz.app.getDataName = function(string) {
    const offset = string.indexOf("-");
    return string.substring(offset + 1);
};

com.kybyz.app.updatePage = function() {
    const cka = com.kybyz.app;
    cka.updateCheck("kbz-posts");
    cka.updateCheck("kbz-messages");
};

com.kybyz.app.updateCheck = function(elementId) {
    const cka = com.kybyz.app;
    let oldContent, newContent, contentHash, xhr;
    if (window.XMLHttpRequest) xhr = new XMLHttpRequest();
    else xhr = new ActiveXObject("Microsoft.XMLHTTP");
    xhr.open("POST", "/update/", true);
    xhr.setRequestHeader('Content-Type',
                         'application/x-www-form-urlencoded');
    oldContent = document.getElementById(elementId);
    contentHash = oldContent.getAttribute("data-version");
    xhr.onreadystatechange = function() {
        if (xhr.readyState == 4 && xhr.status == 200) {
            console.log("result of updateCheck XHR:", xhr.response);
            newContent = xhr.response.body.firstChild;
            if (newContent.getAttribute("id") == elementId)
                oldContent.replaceWith(newContent);
            else console.log("wrong replacement element ID " +
                                 newContent.getAttribute("id") +
                                 " for " + elementId);
        } else {
            console.log("xhr.readyState:", xhr.readyState,
                        ", xhr.status: ", xhr.status);
        }
    };
    xhr.responseType = "document";
    /* NOTE: when you receive a "document" from the backend, even a simple
     * <div>some text</div> gets turned into a full #document.
     * xml.response.documentElement will be the html element, which contains
     * the head, body, and finally the div.
     */
    xhr.send("name=" + cka.getDataName(elementId) + "&hash=" + contentHash);
};

window.addEventListener("load", function(event) {
```

```
    const cka = com.kybyz.app;
    const warning = document.getElementById("kbz-js-warning");
    const text = warning.childNodes[0];
    // NOTE: keep this following string identical to that in kybyz.py
    let fixed = "INFO:found compatible javascript engine";
    const offset = text.data.indexOf(":") + 1;
    fixed = text.data.substring(0, offset) + fixed;
    warning.replaceChild(document.createTextNode(fixed), text);
    window.setInterval(cka.updatePage, cka.UpdateInterval);
});
// vim: tabstop=8 expandtab shiftwidth=4 softtabstop=4
```

4.1.14 kybyz.py

Listing 4.14: kybyz.py

```
#!/usr/bin/python3
'''
Version 0.1 of Kybyz, a peer to peer (p2p) social media platform
'''
# pylint: disable=bad-option-value, consider-using-f-string
import sys, os, math, time, threading  # pylint: disable=multiple-imports
import shlex, re, subprocess  # pylint: disable=multiple-imports
import readline
from socket import fromfd, AF_INET, SOCK_STREAM
from io import BytesIO
from urllib.request import Request, urlopen
from urllib.error import HTTPError
from urllib.parse import parse_qsl
from hashlib import md5
from ircbot import IRCBot
from kbutils import loadposts, registration, cachewrite, guess_mimetype
from kbutils import send, publish, create  # pylint: disable=unused-import
from kbutils import register  # pylint: disable=unused-import
from kbcommon import CACHE, CACHED, logging, MESSAGE_QUEUE, TO_PAGE
from kbcommon import COMMAND, ARGS, read

readline.read_init_file('kybyz_readline.rc')
RUNNING = threading.Event()
CURDIR = os.path.abspath(os.curdir)
REQUEST_COUNT = 0
LOGTIME = int(os.getenv('KB_DELAY', '600'))  # seconds
COMMANDS = ['create', 'register', 'send', 'publish']
NAVIGATION = '<div class="column" id="kbz-navigation">{navigation}</div>'
POSTS = '''<div class="column" id="kbz-posts" data-version="{posts_hash}">
  {posts}
</div>'''
MESSAGES = '''<div class="column" id="kbz-messages"
  data-version="{messages_hash}">
    {messages}
  <div id="kbz-js-warning">webpage:{javascript}</div>
</div>'''
EXPECTED_ERRORS = (  # for repl loop
    RuntimeError,
    KeyError,
    ValueError,
    TypeError,
    AttributeError
)
USER_AGENT = os.getenv(
    'USER_AGENT',
    'Mozilla/5.0 (X11; Linux x86_64; rv:109.0) Gecko/20100101 Firefox/115.0'
)
REMOTE_PORT = int(os.getenv('EXTERNAL_PORT', '-1'))  # request via nginx/tor
KB_USERNAME = os.getenv('KB_USERNAME')
```

```
KB_EMAIL = os.getenv('KB_EMAIL')
HELPERS = {}

def init():
    '''
    initialize application
    '''
    logging.debug('beginning kybyz initialization')
    os.makedirs(CACHE, 0o700, exist_ok=True)
    CACHED.update(registration()._asdict())
    if not CACHED['gpgkey']:
        if KB_USERNAME and KB_EMAIL:
            register(KB_USERNAME, KB_EMAIL)
            CACHED.update(registration()._asdict())
        else:
            logging.error('need to set envvars KB_USERNAME and KB_EMAIL')
    CACHED['uptime'] = 0
    CACHED['javascript'] = 'ERROR:javascript disabled or incompatible'
    logging.debug('CACHED: %s', CACHED)
    RUNNING.set()
    kybyz = threading.Thread(target=background, name='kybyz', daemon=True)
    kybyz.start()
    external_server = threading.Thread(
        target=nginx, name='nginx', daemon=True
    )
    external_server.start()
    if HELPERS.get('nginx'):  # will be non-null if Popen was successful
        punchthrough = threading.Thread(target=tor, name='tor', daemon=True)
        punchthrough.start()
    else:
        logging.error('not starting tor without nginx')

def serve(env=None, start_response=None):
    '''
    handle web requests

    we need at least two dispatchers: one for local use, where requests
    come from the kybyz command line, and from the local browser.

    the other dispatcher is for requests coming from IRC and from the Tor
    network. these must be considered hostile, and there need to be checks
    for friend status and other considerations before deciding what to send.

    the primary exception to the checks is for kybyz.com itself; it can
    (and should?) show its own newsfeed to the world. but should still be
    selective about what it accepts from the world. and rate-limited to avoid
    denial of (service/disk space) attacks.
    '''
    # pylint: disable=too-many-locals, too-many-statements
    global REQUEST_COUNT  # pylint: disable=global-statement
    REQUEST_COUNT += 1
```

```
    env = env or {}
    if REQUEST_COUNT < 1000000:
        logging.debug('env: %s', env)
    # wsgi.input now (as of 2024-12-30 or before) returns bytes object
    wsgi_input = env.get('wsgi.input', BytesIO(b'')).read().decode()
    logging.debug('wsgi.input: %s', wsgi_input)
    args = dict(parse_qsl(wsgi_input))
    logging.debug('args: %s', args)
    page = b'(Something went wrong)'
    requested = env.get('REQUEST_URI', None).lstrip('/')
    server_port = int(env.get('SERVER_PORT', '0'))
    logging.debug('requested: "%s"', requested)
    status = '200 OK'
    headers = [('Content-type', 'text/html')]
    template = read('timeline.html').decode()
    messages = ''.join(['<div>%s</div>' % message for message in
                        reversed(MESSAGE_QUEUE)])
    messages_hash = md5(messages.encode()).hexdigest()
    messages = MESSAGES.format(
        messages=messages,
        messages_hash=messages_hash,
        javascript=CACHED['javascript'])
    posts = ''.join(['<div>%s</div>' % post for post in loadposts()])
    posts_hash = md5(posts.encode()).hexdigest()
    posts = POSTS.format(posts=posts, posts_hash=posts_hash)
    navigation = NAVIGATION.format(navigation=''.join(['<h3>Navigation</h3>']))

    # make helper functions for dispatcher
    def update():
        '''
        process xhr request for update to posts or messages
        '''
        name, hashed = args.get('name', None), args.get('hash', None)
        update_status = status  # default from outer variable
        if name in ('messages', 'posts'):
            # pylint: disable=eval-used
            # check outer variables
            # must be done before eval or it will fail
            logging.debug('messages: ...%s', messages[-128:])
            logging.debug('messages_hash: %s', messages_hash)
            logging.debug('posts: %s...', posts[:128])
            logging.debug('posts_hash: %s', posts_hash)
            if hashed and hashed != eval(name + '_hash'):
                update_page = eval(name).encode()
            elif hashed:
                logging.debug('%s unchanged', name)
                update_page = b''
                update_status = '304 Not Modified'
            else:
                logging.error('no hash passed to /update/')
                update_page = b''
                update_status = '406 Not Acceptable'
        else:
```

```
            update_page = (
                '<div>no updates for %s</div>' % name
            ).encode()
            update_status = '404 Not Found'
        return update_status, update_page

    if requested is not None and start_response:
        if server_port == REMOTE_PORT and KB_USERNAME != 'kybyzdotcom':
            logging.warning('remote request received, env: %s', env)
            status = '501 Not Implemented'
            page = b'<div>Not yet serving remote requests</div>'
        elif requested == '':
            page = template.format(
                posts=posts,
                messages=messages,
                navigation=navigation,
                posts_hash=posts_hash,
                messages_hash=messages_hash,
            ).encode()
        elif os.path.exists(requested):
            page = read(requested)
            headers = [('Content-type', guess_mimetype(requested, page))]
        elif requested.startswith('update/'):
            # assume called by javascript, and thus that it's working
            CACHED['javascript'] = 'INFO:found compatible javascript engine'
            status, page = update()
        elif requested.startswith('ipfs/'):
            url = 'https://ipfs.io/' + requested
            urlrequest = Request(url)
            urlrequest.add_header('user-agent', USER_AGENT)
            logging.debug('fetching uncached ipfs URL %s', url)
            try:
                with urlopen(urlrequest) as request:
                    page = request.read()
                    headers = [
                        ('Content-type', guess_mimetype(requested, page))
                    ]
                cachewrite(requested, page)
            except HTTPError as failed:
                headers = failed.headers.items()
                status = ' '.join([str(failed.code), failed.msg])
                logging.warning('failed fetching %s: %s, %r',
                                url, status, headers)
                page = b'<div>%s</div>' % status.encode()
        else:
            logging.warning('%s not found', requested)
            status = '404 Not Found'
            page = b'<div>not yet implemented</div>'
        # NOTE: page must be a bytestring at this point!
        logging.debug('starting response with status %s and page %s...',
                      status, page[:128])
        start_response(status, headers)
        return [page]
```

```
    logging.warning('serve: failing with env=%s and start_response=%s',
                    env, start_response)
    return [b'']

def get_posts(directory, pattern=None, convert=None):
    '''
    get list of posts

    we use only those symlinked to by unadorned hashes
    '''
    pattern = re.compile(pattern or '^kbz[0-9A-Za-z]*$')
    filenames = [os.path.join(directory, filename)
                 for filename in os.listdir(directory)]
    convert = convert or str  # or specify convert=os.path.realpath
    return [convert(filename)
            for filename in filenames
            if os.path.islink(filename) and pattern.match(filename)]

def background():
    '''
    load and maintain cache

    communicate with other kybyz servers
    '''
    CACHED['ircbot'] = IRCBot(nickname=CACHED.get('username', None))
    # delay must be less than nginx's, and more than 1s
    # (otherwise the `kybyz active %s seconds` display will be doubled)
    delay = 1.1
    while RUNNING.is_set():
        if math.floor(CACHED['uptime']) % LOGTIME == 0:
            logging.info('kybyz active %s seconds',
                         math.floor(CACHED['uptime']), **TO_PAGE)
            logging.debug('CACHED: %s, threads: %s',
                          CACHED, threading.enumerate())
        time.sleep(delay)  # releases the GIL for `serve`
        CACHED['uptime'] += delay
    logging.warning('program stopped, cleaning up...')

def nginx():
    '''
    start nginx to handle external requests via tor
    '''
    # pylint: disable=consider-using-with
    configuration = os.path.join(CURDIR, 'kybyz.conf')
    try:
        HELPERS['nginx'] = subprocess.Popen([
            'nginx',
            '-c', configuration,
            '-e', 'stderr',
            '-g', 'daemon off;'
        ])
        while RUNNING.is_set():
            time.sleep(1.3)  # must be less than tor's
    except FileNotFoundError as failed:
```

```
        logging.error('Failed launching nginx: %s', failed)
    logging.warning('program stopped, nginx terminating...')

def tor():
    '''
    start tor for receiving external requests
    '''
    # pylint: disable=consider-using-with
    try:
        HELPERS['tor'] = subprocess.Popen(['tor', '-f', 'kybyz.torrc'])
        while RUNNING.is_set():
            time.sleep(1.5)
    except FileNotFoundError as failed:
        logging.error('error starting tor: %s', failed)
    logging.warning('program stopped, tor terminating...')

def process(args):
    '''
    process a kybyz command
    '''
    if args and args[0] in COMMANDS:
        print(
            ('result of %s%s:' % (args[0], str(tuple(args[1:])))),
            eval(args[0])(*args[1:]) # pylint: disable=eval-used
    )
    elif args:
        logging.error('must specify one of: %s', COMMANDS)
    else:
        logging.info('no command received to process')

def uwsgi_init():
    '''
    initialize uwsgi application
    '''
    # pylint: disable=import-error, bad-option-value, import-outside-toplevel
    logging.debug('beginning kybyz uwsgi initialization')
    import uwsgi
    if os.getenv('ANDROID_ROOT') is None:
        import webbrowser
    else:
        webbrowser = type(
            '',
            (),
            {'open': lambda url: subprocess.call(['am', 'start', url])}
        )
    port = host = None
    try:
        port = fromfd(uwsgi.sockets[0], AF_INET, SOCK_STREAM).getsockname()[1]
        host = 'kybyz:%s' % port
    except AttributeError:
        logging.exception('cannot determine port')
    init()
```

```
    if not sys.stdin.isatty():
        logging.info('running as background process, will not launch browser')
    else:
        if host is not None and not os.getenv('WSL'):
            logging.debug('opening browser window to %s', host)
            webbrowser.open('http://%s' % host)
        else:
            logging.exception('cannot open browser to %s', host)
            logging.info("if you're running under WSL (Windows Subsystem for"
                         " Linux), just open Windows browser to %s", host)
    repl = threading.Thread(target=commandloop, name='repl', daemon=True)
    repl.start()
    logging.debug('uwsgi initialization complete')

def commandloop():
    '''
    simple repl (read-evaluate-process-loop) for command-line testing
    '''
    time.sleep(10)  # give page a chance to load before starting repl
    args = []
    logging.info('Ready to accept commands; `quit` to terminate input loop')
    while args[0:1] != ['quit']:
        try:
            print(('process%s:' % str(tuple(args))), process(args))
            args = shlex.split(input('kbz> '))
        except EXPECTED_ERRORS:
            logging.exception('command failed, please try again')
            args[:] = []
        except EOFError:
            break
    logging.warning('input loop terminated')

if __name__ == '__main__':
    init()
    process(args=ARGS)
elif COMMAND == 'uwsgi':
    uwsgi_init()
elif COMMAND not in ('pydoc3', 'doctest'):
    logging.info('initalizing on command %s', COMMAND)
    init()
```

4.1.15 kybyz.torrc.template

Listing 4.15: kybyz.torrc.template

```
# see https://community.torproject.org/onion-services/setup/
HiddenServiceDir /tmp/kybyz.tor
HiddenServicePort $EXTERNAL_PORT kybyz:$EXTERNAL_PORT
PidFile $TMPDIR/tor_kybyz.pid
```

4.1.16 kybyzdotcom.pub

Listing 4.16: kybyzdotcom.pub


```
-----BEGIN PGP PUBLIC KEY BLOCK-----

mQGNBGdxuEQBDADEfYr7yLL8+iedd9rZtJmCZ7k2KJCd3R5CkPTJdD5rhQURh+yp
v5bWkoqLAwWUk1IH7Q2iW5/e8cued/GCBv4Z72OJKdhQmq3vs7pxiEZtWc4B79PW
HpQcbYb7ouJXwM16b2GcET2vn9xMaUeVbpePiAr5OiRiLZjDceevzjWyqq/MQ1Xz
zfct1vbWwlqJml2mvuIsvhuSEpf0zOUqJ6Xlo7unDQ8TtlVEA2YpBSU0IX8tdpal
U1ecVBw5Q9BiDHqepca+w3IwRL9+4zJl3eKvfKLTo8VoMxxyanBizrGQaofBCIGb
qTxOtSGjJggx+5eAs3k/Qxy88f5RSTtk53QODzj1txSe2GWsnahO/t0ABrcAQXgd
t13+ifFQ1F4eli0DtThtwMkhA00QKmvU7F7BX8BvDbjKatRT3OgwVhCQfGYg9G9t
5+cGvCXPlEwl7J6Yvwze4ysJemYAYjLk+5pxLUpmQK55XjGZgXEQfbbupoWYKXzX
cazQC9CkSZnf+58AEQEAAbQda3lieXpkb3Rjb20gPGt5Ynl6QGt5Ynl6LmNvbT6J
Ac4EEwEKADgWIQQ0F2TN/VLBiDLimjkRCGHNv6KXEwUCZ3G4RAIbAwULCQgHAgYV
CgkICwIEFgIDAQIeAQIXgAAKCRARCGHNv6KXE9zsC/9uiYHfsJFEGSFNTf1l/xKP
OXVhBYgvoGR/1ejsSOOtx34B8SJicGlCBzNvdZc5tO6DUs5Uvghosjlje3ZDPeBs
kN5rM755Fe9yBBxxNrqRGuwknzd2vScnrEJ5kMSsZ385myP+USeOVTaiPP8bqXUA
JnXtYZ2wrOJx8ctj7MDdYW1bx2wrgX+yfE1j+STBhhOTZhoTDRMblW6OIegriRp/
8L5O5OvJ9b+4tEjYiki8lBIresL/vjNlL1hJLE7Wq3jcwdmpySZz4zJic+nuu0hZ
Olv3oB5zou2GxjN1Bbo7BfT11PZtycMXRblOkRxx0iWGRNwwPpgVx5DWeuPmVgaa
AHNEjkGPxdn6kSMJDZ99V+wCG5mkBF1+0+nhvHq4B7nGiAkrI9UZpCiOCq1N82TI
pArytHjOxl1THb6B8/ALCyv0Lt8A0hwSV6eSmaKUOa0B45fTCy7VN59YdMuUzIlK
kbqnkRAA0t8BdnqW+lVuO2T9xy4qZU1bvM90Jz87Za65AY0EZ3G4RAEMAL/FAnQM
B0RwAkBA1zZMpXRFxDqUUprxre8P0HE7NAtKSsIujLj+UxX/5Sl3AMEEmG+bD7q2
OJV9lr80O+vEWg4rKd4WQF6QYrCc6Ya+4O8a/aILHAhPqUOlJVAVG7a70u5LQahR
mzq4YLVbwpMGBcDGGsOKfho350wfQCSURVIhg2HsbtPoCIRz1N8q0ljwP3YtTwNX
7rR44hyOoPdukTyM4JnNBa8tNXxuHJ2aycAWSCQ7/2VmOfOMcKWjb6yWIARu6iaY
PE6V63FiQ+7gSE0EWcqD+ITETGhV+o9GZaG2yOY4f7fB4E1qXqlxGB4R5aYq9xiY
992jS9SH0mBxL4RjLoTia81W6GHi5RQ9mlo8wNtMlnQmItL4FWVZ4g3WjmfpcOwX
i+81OePwiySx8txne/w/JLyxVcK2TiLqqCpZCef+tAndeA00YgK4GWZqqAqf6KfG
LMnnWgk86jfm1CZj+VkyULbiFX/8VnI6whqznYuAAi9+4vFYa1IdBoDB4wARAQAB
iQG2BBgBCgAgFiEENBdkzf1SwYgy4po5EQhhzb+ilxMFAmdxuEQCGwwACgkQEQhh
zb+ilxPhUgwAw8UZZCw7lmLI8jhHMeKwHuVdd6D0/3tggO6C3VSCcxtnLDf1645m
mVtK+Mdaj0I0yrRe5i3yiXuJowVT0JIlDyXc+qg6t8phGVeMv/edJ5Ha56HwQbbK
18DThb9CM2bXMXYnPSMYUI1A103Pz7+IPCP/Zk6wRtRF+UpuKz23180XM3RqvppZ
DIweqyqSl9+5/dTMtdxyvPjmubGEpIDgZ2TlPEg2vhbgts0Cy4Ux22cPYONOuuYq
yGcqLHinhN9SMdLenLWxqNXwmouDaNk+auD/64BeDR7kgJTOTxzOHgsBoA0cOYRA
W1VwSVtxdsNAZJOdP29mwnf/Q/SE/VJLj/+Rb8xv90uFD4yZgMJ4IFSv6nx4A0Th
eXTwkj4agFx1a7Gm4raH11hTqU00dOmNSIgVbABtbC9xonSS8opCkivs1FInVJqf
Ct5b/6KeJsXHF2wRKjzBNNej9V8kjjF5OQhQcgYTWujgfe8PcHO3E9adJYPmjLnb
SnaMYEGiKugA
=LueN
-----END PGP PUBLIC KEY BLOCK-----
```

4.1.17 linux.mk

Listing 4.17: linux.mk

```
# set shell to Bash to allow use of bashisms in recipes
# 'make SHELL='/bin/bash -x'' to debug Makefile
SHELL := /bin/bash
APP := $(notdir $(PWD))
SOURCES ?= $(wildcard *.py)
INSTALLER ?= $(shell command -v yum || command -v apt-get || command -v echo)
REQUIRED := chromium gpg
PKG_REQUIRED := uwsgi-plugin-python3 python3-gnupg pylint3
PIP_REQUIRED := uwsgi python-gnupg pylint
USER_BIN ?= $(HOME)/.local/bin
USER_LOG ?= $(HOME)/.local/log
PYTHON ?= $(shell which python3 python python2 false | head -n 1)
PIP ?= $(shell which pip3 pip pip2 false | head -n 1)
PYLINT ?= $(shell which pylint3 pylint pylint2 true | head -n 1)
PY_VER := $(shell $(PYTHON) -c "import sys; print(sys.version_info[0])")
ifeq ($(PY_VER),3)
 REQUIRED += $(PKG_REQUIRED)
endif
# set KB_DELAY to smaller number for more frequent progress logging
KB_DELAY ?= 600
# set KB_LOGDIR to desired path
# it will be created by kbcommon.py at startup
KB_LOGDIR := $(USER_LOG)
PATH := $(USER_BIN):$(PATH)
# set fixed port of 26351 derived from base36 of 'kbz'
KB_WEB := $(shell $(PYTHON) -c "print(int('kbz', 36))")
KB_COMMS := $(shell expr $(KB_WEB) + 1)
TMPDIR := $(shell $(PYTHON) -c "import tempfile; print(tempfile.gettempdir())")
ONION_FILE := /tmp/kybyz.tor/hostname
ONION_ADDR = $(shell test -e $(ONION_FILE) && cat $(ONION_FILE))
EXTERNAL_PORT := 8008
ONION_URL := http://$(ONION_ADDR):$(EXTERNAL_PORT)
ifeq ($(SHOWENV),)
export APP KB_DELAY KB_WEB KB_LOGDIR KB_COMMS TMPDIR EXTERNAL_PORT USER_LOG
else
export
endif
all: $(PYLINT) doctests lint kybyz.conf kybyz.torrc uwsgi
%.doctest: %.py
	$(PYTHON) -m doctest $<
doctests: $(SOURCES:.py=.doctest)
%.lint %.pylint: %.py
	$(PYLINT) $<
lint pylint: $(SOURCES:.py=.lint)
install:  # run first as root, then as user
	if [ -w / ]; then \
	 $(INSTALLER) update; \
	 command -v python3 || command -v python || \
```

```
	  $(INSTALLER) install python3 || $(INSTALLER) install python; \
	  command -v pip3 || command -v pip || \
	  $(INSTALLER) install python3-pip || $(INSTALLER) install python-pip; \
	  $(INSTALLER) install $(REQUIRED); \
	 else \
	  for package in $(PIP_REQUIRED); do \
	   command -v $$package || \
	   $(PYTHON) -c "import $${package##python-}" || \
	   $(PIP) install --user $$package; \
	  done; \
	 fi
uwsgi: kybyz.ini resources/vis-network.min.js
	#strace -f -v -t -s4096 -o $(TMPDIR)/kybyz_strace.log uwsgi $<
	# don't '2>&1', it may affect prompt display
	uwsgi $<
nginx: $(PWD)/kybyz.conf
	nginx -c $< -e stderr &
nginx.stop:
	if [ -e /tmp/nginx_kybyz.pid ]; then \
	 if [ "$$(</tmp/nginx_kybyz.pid)" ]; then \
	  kill $$(</tmp/nginx_kybyz.pid); \
	 else \
	  echo 'found nginx pidfile empty' >&2; \
	 fi; \
	 rm -f /tmp/nginx_kybyz.pid; \
	else \
	 echo 'nginx already not running' >&2; \
	fi
tor: kybyz.torrc
	tor -f $< &
tor.stop:
	if [ -e /tmp/tor_kybyz.pid ]; then \
	 if [ "$$(</tmp/tor_kybyz.pid)" ]; then \
	  kill $$(</tmp/tor_kybyz.pid); \
	 else \
	  echo 'found tor pidfile empty' >&2; \
	 fi; \
	 rm -f /tmp/tor_kybyz.pid; \
	else \
	 echo 'tor already not running' >&2; \
	fi
stop:
	if [ -e /tmp/kybyz.pid ]; then \
	 if [ "$$(</tmp/kybyz.pid)" ]; then \
	  kill $$(</tmp/kybyz.pid); \
	 else \
	  echo 'found kybyz pidfile empty' >&2; \
	 fi; \
	 rm -f /tmp/kybyz.pid; \
	else \
	 echo 'kybyz already not running' >&2; \
	fi
strace:
```

```
	if [ -e /tmp/kybyz.pid ]; then \
	 strace -p $$(</tmp/kybyz.pid) \
	  -f -v -s128 -o '| tee /tmp/kybyz_strace.log'; \
	else \
	 echo cannot find pid of kybyz process >&2; \
	fi
$(USER_BIN):
	mkdir -p $@
$(PYLINT): $(USER_BIN)
	# assuming either pylint3 or pylint available
	command -v $(PYLINT) || \
	ln -s $$(command -v pylint3 || command -v pylint) $</$@
env:
ifeq ($(SHOWENV),)
	make SHOWENV=1 $@
else
	$@
endif
edit: k*.py
	vi $+
torview:
	torbrowser-launcher $(ONION_URL)
kybyz.service: service.template
	envsubst < $< > $@
kybyz.conf: nginx.conf.template
	envsubst < $< > $@
kybyz.torrc: kybyz.torrc.template linux.mk
	envsubst < $< > $@
push:
	git push -u origin master
	git push githost master
resources/vis-network.min.js:
	cd $(@D) && \
	 wget https://unpkg.com/vis-network/standalone/umd/$(@F)
```

4.1.18 netmeme.css

Listing 4.18: netmeme.css

```
/* codepen.io/MetalEscape/pen/WrYxVM */
* {
  box-sizing: border-box;
}

.netmeme {
  margin: auto;
  width: 100%;
  aspect-ratio: 1;
  background-size: cover;
  text-align: center;
  position: relative;
}

.netmeme p {
  position: absolute;
  left: 0;
  right: 0;
  margin: 15px 0;
  padding: 0 5px;
  font-family: impact;
  font-size: 2.5em;
  color: white;
  letter-spacing: 1px;
  text-shadow:2px 2px 0 #000,
    -2px -2px 0 #000,
    2px -2px 0 #000,
    -2px 2px 0 #000,
    0px 2px 0 #000,
    2px 0px 0 #000,
    0px -2px 0 #000,
    -2px 0px 0 #000;
}

.bottom {
  bottom: 0;
}

.top {
  top: 0;
}
```

4.1.19 netmeme.html

Listing 4.19: netmeme.html

```
<div class="netmeme" style="background-image: url('{post.image}')">
  <p class="top">{post.toptext}</p>
  <p class="bottom">{post.bottomtext}</p>
</div>
```

4.1.20 network.html

Listing 4.20: network.html

```
<!doctype html>
<html lang="en">
<head>
  <meta charset="utf-8">
  <title>kybyz homepage</title>
  <link rel="stylesheet" href="network.css">
</head>
<body>
</body>
</html>
```

4.1.21 nginx.conf.template

Listing 4.21: nginx.conf.template

```
# from nginx.org/en/docs/example.html as of 2025-01-02
# (only need 'user' directive if starting as root)
#user $USER $USER;
worker_processes 1;
pid $TMPDIR/nginx_$APP.pid;
events {
	worker_connections 10;
}
http {
	server {
		listen $EXTERNAL_PORT;
		server_name $APP $APP.com www.$APP.com;
		charset utf-8;
		access_log $USER_LOG/kybyz_nginx.access.log;
		location / {
			include /etc/nginx/uwsgi_params;
			uwsgi_pass unix://$TMPDIR/$APP.sock;
		}
	}
}
```

4.1.22 post.css

Listing 4.22: post.css

```
.post {
  margin: auto;
  width: 100%;
  max-aspect-ratio: 1/1;
  text-align: left;
  position: relative;
}

.bottom {
  bottom: 0;
}

.top {
  top: 0;
}
```

4.1.23 post.html

Listing 4.23: post.html

```
<div class="post">
  <p class="top">{post.toptext}</p>
  <div class="imagebox"><img src="{post.image}"</img></div>
  <p class="bottom">{post.bottomtext}</p>
</div>
```

4.1.24 post.py

Listing 4.24: post.py

```
#!/usr/bin/python3
'''
kybyz post
'''
# pylint: disable=bad-option-value, consider-using-f-string
import os, json, re  # pylint: disable=multiple-imports
from kbcommon import read, make_timestamp, tuplify, logging, CACHED, \
 doctestdebug
from canonical_json import canonicalize
LIKE = '\N{THUMBS UP SIGN}'
LOVE = '\N{BLACK HEART SUIT}'

class PostValidationError(ValueError):  # pylint: disable=too-few-public-methods
    '''
    distinguish validation errors from other ValueErrors
    '''

class NoDefault():  # pylint: disable=too-few-public-methods
    '''
    distinguish attributes with no defaults from None
    '''

class PostAttribute():
    '''
    base class for kybyz post attributes
    '''
    def __init__(self, name, required=True, hashed=True, values=None):
        '''
        post attributes have unique names

        required can be:
            True,
            False,
            a tuple evaluated as names of other post attributes that must be
            present and evaluate to True; for example, mimetype is dependent on
            there being an image, so mimetype's `required` value would be
            ('image',),
            a list of names of other post attributes, at least one of which
            (including the attribute having this `required` value) must be
            present and evaluate to True (NOTE: new in v0.0.2),
            or any other object which fits `values`, which will be used as
            the default, and required therefore presumed to be True.

        hashed can be:
            True,
            False (both key and value removed before hashing),
            None (set to None (null) before hashing),
```

```
            or a particular value (such as [] to empty a list before hashing)

        values can be a tuple of allowed values, None to allow any value,
        a re.Pattern to specify a match pattern (implying str object), or
        a lambda expression that must return True for the value to be valid.
        '''
        self.name = name
        self.required = required
        self.hashed = hashed
        self.values = values

    def validate(self, post):
        '''
        make sure this attribute fits requirement

        NOTE: sets attribute in post if not present and has default value
        '''
        def validate_tuple(value):
            '''
            helper function for values tuple
            '''
            doctestdebug('validating that value %r in %s', value, self.values)
            return value in self.values

        def validate_pattern(value):
            '''
            helper function for values as compiled regex
            '''
            doctestdebug('validating pattern %s matches value %r',
                         self.values, value)
            try:
                return self.values.match(value)
            except TypeError as error:
                raise PostValidationError(
                    '%r is wrong type for pattern match %s' % (value, self)
                ) from error

        def validate_none(value):  # pylint: disable=unused-argument
            '''
            helper function for value that can be anything
            '''
            doctestdebug('validating %r regardless of what it is', value)
            return True

        def validate_lambda(value):
            '''
            helper function for values as lambda expression
            '''
            doctestdebug('validating lambda expression %s(%r)',
                         self.values, value)
```

```
            return self.values(value)

        validation_dispatcher = {
            type(None): validate_none,
            type(re.compile(r'^$')): validate_pattern,
            type(lambda: None): validate_lambda,
            type(()): validate_tuple,
        }

        required = self.required
        default = NoDefault
        if isinstance(required, tuple):
            evaluated = all((getattr(post, attribute, None)
                             for attribute in required))
            doctestdebug('tuple %s evaluated to required=%s',
                         required, evaluated)
            required = evaluated
        elif required not in [True, False]:
            doctestdebug('setting default for %s to %r', self.name,
            required)
            default = required
            required = True
        value = getattr(post, self.name, default)
        doctestdebug('checking that %s value %r in %s',
                     self.name, value, self.values)
        validation_dispatcher[type(self.values)](value)
        if value == NoDefault and required:
            raise PostValidationError('Post %r lacks valid %s attribute' %
                                      (post, self.name))
        if value != NoDefault:
            doctestdebug('setting attribute %s in post to %s',
                         self.name, value)
            setattr(post, self.name, value)  # default if nothing else
        else:
            doctestdebug('attribute %s has value %r and no default value',
                         self.name, value)

    def hashvalue(self, post):
        '''
        return key and value for hashing

        if post lacks attribute at this point, return invalid (None, None)
        '''
        try:
            value = getattr(post, self.name)
            if self.hashed is False:
                raise AttributeError(
                    '%s not part of post hashvalue' % self.name
                )
        except AttributeError:
            return (None, None)
        if self.hashed is True:
            return (self.name, value)
        # None or any other explicit value
```

```
        return (self.name, self.hashed)

    def __str__(self):
        return '<PostAttribute name=%r required=%r hashed=%r values=%r>' % (
            self.name, self.required, self.hashed, self.values)
    __repr__ = __str__

class BasePost():
    '''
    base class for kybyz posts
    '''
    classname = 'basepost'
    versions = {
        '0.0.1': {
            'basepost': {
                'type': PostAttribute('type', values=(
                    'post', 'netmeme', 'kybyz', 'resource')
                ),
                'version': PostAttribute('version', values=('0.0.1',)),
                'author': PostAttribute(
                    'author',
                    values=re.compile(r'^\w+[\w\s]*\w$')
                ),
                'fingerprint': PostAttribute(
                    'fingerprint',
                    values=re.compile(r'^[0-9A-F]{16}$')),
                'image': PostAttribute('image', required=''),
                'mimetype': PostAttribute('mimetype', required=('image',)),
                'toptext': PostAttribute('toptext', required=''),
                'bottomtext': PostAttribute('bottomtext', required=''),
                'signed': PostAttribute('signed', required=False),
                'timestamp': PostAttribute('timestamp', hashed=False),
                'in-reply-to': PostAttribute('in-reply-to',
                                             required=False,
                                             hashed=[],
                                             values=lambda v: isinstance(
                                                 v, list)
                                             ),
                'replies': PostAttribute('replies',
                                         required=False,
                                         hashed=[],
                                         values=lambda v: isinstance(v, list)),
            }
        }
    }
    versions['0.0.1']['kybyz'] = dict(versions['0.0.1']['basepost'].items())
    versions['0.0.1']['kybyz']['text'] = PostAttribute('text', required=LIKE)
    del versions['0.0.1']['kybyz']['toptext']
    del versions['0.0.1']['kybyz']['bottomtext']
```

```
    versions['0.0.1']['post'] = dict(versions['0.0.1']['basepost'].items())
    versions['0.0.1']['netmeme'] = dict(versions['0.0.1']['basepost'].items())
    versions['0.0.1']['resource'] = dict(versions['0.0.1']['basepost'].items())
    versions['0.0.1']['resource']['ipfs_id'] = PostAttribute(
        'ipfs_id', required=True)
    versions['0.0.1']['resource']['source_uri'] = PostAttribute(
        'source_uri', required=False)
    versions['0.0.1']['resource']['identifier'] = PostAttribute(
        'identifier', required=True)
    def __new__(cls, filename='', **kwargs):
        '''
        previous approach was failing, since changes made to kwargs in __new__
        don't make it into __init__.

        the *only reason* for __new__ is to be able to instantiate the
        right subclass of BasePost without having to duplicate code into
        each subclass. but to do that, it may need to fill in kwargs from
        a file or from other sources. at the very least, it needs the
        post_type, which points to the subclass, and the version number.

        the idea behind version numbers is that, as the code grows and
        semantics change, old posts can still be recognized and rendered.
        '''
        if not kwargs:
            try:
                kwargs.update(json.loads(read(filename)))
            except TypeError as failed:
                logging.error('no keywords supplied,'
                              ' and file %r cannot be read: %s',
                              filename, failed)
                return None
        doctestdebug('type: %s, cls: %s, cls.classname: %s',
                     kwargs.get('type'), cls, cls.classname)
        post_type = kwargs.get('type', cls.classname)
        # if no version specified, use latest
        default_version = max(cls.versions, key=tuplify)
        version = kwargs.get('version', default_version)
        if filename and post_type not in MAPPING:
            post_type = os.path.splitext(filename)[1].lstrip('.')
        subclass = MAPPING.get(post_type, cls)
        doctestdebug('updated kwargs: %s, subclass: %s', kwargs, subclass)
        try:
            # pylint: disable=no-value-for-parameter  # (why? dunno)
            instance = super().__new__(subclass)
            # fill in defaults from things unknown at script load time
            instance.versions[version][post_type]['author'].required = \
                CACHED.get('username', True)
            instance.versions[version][post_type]['fingerprint'].required = \
                CACHED.get('gpgkey', '')[-16:] or True
```

```
        except TypeError:
            logging.exception('Unknown post type %s', subclass)
            instance = None
        return instance

    def __init__(self, filename='', **kwargs):
        '''
        initialize instantiation from file or from kwargs and defaults
        '''
        if not kwargs:
            kwargs = json.loads(read(filename))
        logging.debug('%s.__init__(): kwargs=%s',
                      MAPPING[self.classname], kwargs)
        for key in kwargs:
            setattr(self, key, kwargs[key])
        if not getattr(self, 'timestamp', None):
            self.timestamp = make_timestamp()
        if not getattr(self, 'type', None):
            self.type = self.classname
        # if no version specified, use latest
        if not getattr(self, 'version', None):
            self.version = max(self.versions, key=tuplify)
        self.validate()

    def __str__(self):
        '''
        return string representation
        '''
        return self.to_html()

    def validate(self):
        '''
        make sure post contents fit the version given

        note that additional attributes can be given a post and they
        will not be checked; we only check the schema
        '''
        if not self.__doc__:
            raise RuntimeError('Must not run with optimization')
        # why doesn't 'author' have default value from cache?
        doctestdebug('BasePost.validate: CACHED: %s', CACHED)
        assert (getattr(self, 'type', None) == self.classname or
                getattr(self, 'filename', '').endswith('.' + self.classname))
        schema = self.versions[self.version][self.type]
        doctestdebug('post validation schema: %s', schema)
        for attribute in schema:
            doctestdebug('validating attribute %s in schema', attribute)
            schema[attribute].validate(self)

    def to_html(self):
        '''
        output contents as HTML
        '''
```

```
        template = read(self.classname + '.html').decode()
        return template.format(post=self)

    def to_json(self, for_hashing=False):
        '''
        output contents as JSON
        '''
        if for_hashing:
            dictionary = dict((value.hashvalue(self) for value in
                               self.versions[self.version][self.type].values()))
            del dictionary[None]  # clears out last of values not to be hashed
        else:
            dictionary = self.__dict__
            logging.warning('dictionary: %s', dictionary)
        return canonicalize(dictionary)

class Post(BasePost):
    r'''
    encapsulation of kybyz post

    >>> str(Post(author='test',
    ...          fingerprint='0000000000000000'))  # doctest: +ELLIPSIS
    '<div class="post">\n...'
    '''
    classname = 'post'

class Netmeme(BasePost):
    '''
    encapsulation of kybyz Internet meme (netmeme is my abbreviation)
    '''
    classname = 'netmeme'

class Kybyz(BasePost):
    '''
    encapsulation of a "kybyz": a "thumbs-up" or other icon with optional text
    '''
    classname = 'kybyz'

class Resource(BasePost):
    '''
    add a book, article, movie, or any digital resource to IPFS, and name it
    '''
    classname='resource'

MAPPING = {subclass.classname: subclass
           for subclass in BasePost.__subclasses__()}

if __name__ == '__main__':
    logging.info('MAPPING: %s', MAPPING)
    logging.debug('testing post')
```

```
    print(BasePost('example.kybyz/testmeme.json'))
# vim: tabstop=8 expandtab shiftwidth=4 softtabstop=4
```

4.1.25 service.template

Listing 4.25: service.template

```
[Unit]
Description=Kybyz monitor, specifically for kybyz.com

[Service]
User=$USER
Group=$USER
WorkingDirectory=$PWD
ExecStart=make

[Install]
WantedBy=multi-user.target
```

4.1.26 testpage.html

Listing 4.26: testpage.html

```
<!DOCTYPE html>
<html lang="en">
  <head>
    <title>kybyz testpage</title>
    <script type="text/javascript" src="resources/vis-network.minjs"></
    script>
    <style type="text/css">
        #mynetwork {
            width: 100%;
            height: 100%;
        }
    </style>
  </head>
  <body>
    <h1>kybyz example</h1>
    <div id="mynetwork"></div>
    <script type="text/javascript">
      function startNetwork(data) {
        const container = document.getElementById("mynetwork");
        const options = {};
        new vis.Network(container, data, options);
      }
      const nodes = new vis.DataSet([
        { id: 1, label: "Eric Cartman", age: "kid", gender: "male" },
        { id: 2, label: "Stan Marsh", age: "kid", gender: "male" },
        { id: 3, label: "Wendy Testaburger", age: "kid", gender: "female"
        },
        { id: 4, label: "Mr Mackey", age: "adult", gender: "male" },
        { id: 5, label: "Sharon Marsh", age: "adult", gender: "female" },
      ]);
      const edges = new vis.DataSet([
        {
          from: 1,
          to: 2,
          relation: "friend",
          arrows: "to, from",
          color: { color: "red" },
        },
        {
          from: 1,
          to: 3,
          relation: "friend",
          arrows: "to, from",
          color: { color: "red" },
        },
        {
          from: 2,
          to: 3,
          relation: "friend",
          arrows: "to, from",
          color: { color: "red" },
```

```
        },
        {
          from: 5,
          to: 2,
          relation: "parent",
          arrows: "to",
          color: { color: "green" },
        },
        {
          from: 5,
          to: 2,
          relation: "parent",
          arrows: "from,to",
          color: { color: "purple" },
        },
        {
          from: 4,
          to: 1,
          relation: "teacher",
          arrows: "to",
          color: { color: "blue" },
        },
        {
          from: 4,
          to: 2,
          relation: "teacher",
          arrows: "to",
          color: { color: "blue" },
        },
        {
          from: 4,
          to: 3,
          relation: "teacher",
          arrows: "to",
          color: { color: "blue" },
        },
      ]);
      const nodesView = new vis.DataView(nodes);
      const edgesView = new vis.DataView(edges);
      startNetwork({ nodes: nodesView, edges: edgesView });
    </script>
  </body>
</html>
```

4.1.27 timeline.css

Listing 4.27: timeline.css

```
.column {
        float: left;
        width: 33.3%;
}

#kbz-navigation, #kbz-messages {
        padding: 1em;
}

/* https://css-tricks.com/snippets/css/clear-fix/ */
.row:after {
        content: "";
        display: table;
        clear: both;
}
```

4.1.28 timeline.html

Listing 4.28: timeline.html

```
<!doctype html>
<html lang="en">
<head>
  <meta charset="utf-8">
  <title>kybyz homepage</title>
  <link rel="stylesheet" href="timeline.css">
  <link rel="stylesheet" href="post.css">
  <link rel="stylesheet" href="netmeme.css">
  <script type="text/javascript" src="kybyz.js"></script>
</head>
<body>
<div class="row">
  {navigation}
  {posts}
  {messages}
</div>
</body>
</html>
```

4.2 Subdirectory example.kybyz/

4.2.1 example.kybyz/testmeme.json

Listing 4.29: example.kybyz/testmeme.json


```
{"type":"netmeme","version":"0.0.1","author":"jcomeauictx","fingerprint
":"37AA2CDDD6EECB96","image":"ipfs/
QmW2WQi7j6c7UgJTarActp7tDNikE4B2qXtFCfLPdsgaTQ/cat.jpg","mimetype":"image/
jpeg","timestamp":"2021-09-13T16:35:32.440165+00:00","toptext":"","
bottomtext":"I kan haz cheezburger?","signed":null,"in_reply_to":[],"
replies":[]}
```

4.3 Subdirectory kybyz.com/

4.3.1 kybyz.com/Makefile

Listing 4.30: kybyz.com/Makefile

```
WEBSITE ?= $(notdir $(PWD))
DRYRUN ?= --dry-run
DOCROOT := /var/www/$(WEBSITE)
upload:
	rsync -avuz $(DRYRUN) \
	 --exclude=Makefile \
	 --exclude=README.md \
	 . $(WEBSITE):$(DOCROOT)/
```

4.3.2 kybyz.com/index.html

Listing 4.31: kybyz.com/index.html

```
<p>
Placeholder for kybyz.com
<p>
See sources at <a href="https://github.com/jcomeauictx/kybyz">github</a>.
```

4.4 Subdirectory kybyz_v0/

4.4.1 kybyz_v0/LICENSE

Listing 4.32: kybyz_v0/LICENSE

```
                    GNU GENERAL PUBLIC LICENSE
                       Version 3, 29 June 2007

 Copyright (C) 2007 Free Software Foundation, Inc. <http://fsf.org/>
 Everyone is permitted to copy and distribute verbatim copies
 of this license document, but changing it is not allowed.

                            Preamble

  The GNU General Public License is a free, copyleft license for
software and other kinds of works.

  The licenses for most software and other practical works are designed
to take away your freedom to share and change the works.  By contrast,
the GNU General Public License is intended to guarantee your freedom to
share and change all versions of a program--to make sure it remains free
software for all its users.  We, the Free Software Foundation, use the
GNU General Public License for most of our software; it applies also to
any other work released this way by its authors.  You can apply it to
your programs, too.

  When we speak of free software, we are referring to freedom, not
price.  Our General Public Licenses are designed to make sure that you
have the freedom to distribute copies of free software (and charge for
them if you wish), that you receive source code or can get it if you
want it, that you can change the software or use pieces of it in new
free programs, and that you know you can do these things.

  To protect your rights, we need to prevent others from denying you
these rights or asking you to surrender the rights.  Therefore, you have
certain responsibilities if you distribute copies of the software, or if
you modify it: responsibilities to respect the freedom of others.

  For example, if you distribute copies of such a program, whether
gratis or for a fee, you must pass on to the recipients the same
freedoms that you received.  You must make sure that they, too, receive
or can get the source code.  And you must show them these terms so they
know their rights.

  Developers that use the GNU GPL protect your rights with two steps:
(1) assert copyright on the software, and (2) offer you this License
giving you legal permission to copy, distribute and/or modify it.

  For the developers' and authors' protection, the GPL clearly explains
that there is no warranty for this free software.  For both users' and
authors' sake, the GPL requires that modified versions be marked as
changed, so that their problems will not be attributed erroneously to
authors of previous versions.

  Some devices are designed to deny users access to install or run
modified versions of the software inside them, although the manufacturer
```

```
can do so.  This is fundamentally incompatible with the aim of
protecting users' freedom to change the software.  The systematic
pattern of such abuse occurs in the area of products for individuals to
use, which is precisely where it is most unacceptable.  Therefore, we
have designed this version of the GPL to prohibit the practice for those
products.  If such problems arise substantially in other domains, we
stand ready to extend this provision to those domains in future versions
of the GPL, as needed to protect the freedom of users.

  Finally, every program is threatened constantly by software patents.
States should not allow patents to restrict development and use of
software on general-purpose computers, but in those that do, we wish to
avoid the special danger that patents applied to a free program could
make it effectively proprietary.  To prevent this, the GPL assures that
patents cannot be used to render the program non-free.

  The precise terms and conditions for copying, distribution and
modification follow.

                       TERMS AND CONDITIONS

  0. Definitions.

  "This License" refers to version 3 of the GNU General Public License.

  "Copyright" also means copyright-like laws that apply to other kinds of
works, such as semiconductor masks.

  "The Program" refers to any copyrightable work licensed under this
License.  Each licensee is addressed as "you".  "Licensees" and
"recipients" may be individuals or organizations.

  To "modify" a work means to copy from or adapt all or part of the work
in a fashion requiring copyright permission, other than the making of an
exact copy.  The resulting work is called a "modified version" of the
earlier work or a work "based on" the earlier work.

  A "covered work" means either the unmodified Program or a work based
on the Program.

  To "propagate" a work means to do anything with it that, without
permission, would make you directly or secondarily liable for
infringement under applicable copyright law, except executing it on a
computer or modifying a private copy.  Propagation includes copying,
distribution (with or without modification), making available to the
public, and in some countries other activities as well.

  To "convey" a work means any kind of propagation that enables other
parties to make or receive copies.  Mere interaction with a user through
a computer network, with no transfer of a copy, is not conveying.

  An interactive user interface displays "Appropriate Legal Notices"
to the extent that it includes a convenient and prominently visible
feature that (1) displays an appropriate copyright notice, and (2)
```

```
tells the user that there is no warranty for the work (except to the
extent that warranties are provided), that licensees may convey the
work under this License, and how to view a copy of this License.  If
the interface presents a list of user commands or options, such as a
menu, a prominent item in the list meets this criterion.

  1. Source Code.

  The "source code" for a work means the preferred form of the work
for making modifications to it.  "Object code" means any non-source
form of a work.

  A "Standard Interface" means an interface that either is an official
standard defined by a recognized standards body, or, in the case of
interfaces specified for a particular programming language, one that
is widely used among developers working in that language.

  The "System Libraries" of an executable work include anything, other
than the work as a whole, that (a) is included in the normal form of
packaging a Major Component, but which is not part of that Major
Component, and (b) serves only to enable use of the work with that
Major Component, or to implement a Standard Interface for which an
implementation is available to the public in source code form.  A
"Major Component", in this context, means a major essential component
(kernel, window system, and so on) of the specific operating system
(if any) on which the executable work runs, or a compiler used to
produce the work, or an object code interpreter used to run it.

  The "Corresponding Source" for a work in object code form means all
the source code needed to generate, install, and (for an executable
work) run the object code and to modify the work, including scripts to
control those activities.  However, it does not include the work's
System Libraries, or general-purpose tools or generally available free
programs which are used unmodified in performing those activities but
which are not part of the work.  For example, Corresponding Source
includes interface definition files associated with source files for
the work, and the source code for shared libraries and dynamically
linked subprograms that the work is specifically designed to require,
such as by intimate data communication or control flow between those
subprograms and other parts of the work.

  The Corresponding Source need not include anything that users
can regenerate automatically from other parts of the Corresponding
Source.

  The Corresponding Source for a work in source code form is that
same work.

  2. Basic Permissions.

  All rights granted under this License are granted for the term of
copyright on the Program, and are irrevocable provided the stated
conditions are met.  This License explicitly affirms your unlimited
permission to run the unmodified Program.  The output from running a
```

```
covered work is covered by this License only if the output, given its
content, constitutes a covered work.  This License acknowledges your
rights of fair use or other equivalent, as provided by copyright law.

  You may make, run and propagate covered works that you do not
convey, without conditions so long as your license otherwise remains
in force.  You may convey covered works to others for the sole purpose
of having them make modifications exclusively for you, or provide you
with facilities for running those works, provided that you comply with
the terms of this License in conveying all material for which you do
not control copyright.  Those thus making or running the covered works
for you must do so exclusively on your behalf, under your direction
and control, on terms that prohibit them from making any copies of
your copyrighted material outside their relationship with you.

  Conveying under any other circumstances is permitted solely under
the conditions stated below.  Sublicensing is not allowed; section 10
makes it unnecessary.

  3. Protecting Users' Legal Rights From Anti-Circumvention Law.

  No covered work shall be deemed part of an effective technological
measure under any applicable law fulfilling obligations under article
11 of the WIPO copyright treaty adopted on 20 December 1996, or
similar laws prohibiting or restricting circumvention of such
measures.

  When you convey a covered work, you waive any legal power to forbid
circumvention of technological measures to the extent such circumvention
is effected by exercising rights under this License with respect to
the covered work, and you disclaim any intention to limit operation or
modification of the work as a means of enforcing, against the work's
users, your or third parties' legal rights to forbid circumvention of
technological measures.

  4. Conveying Verbatim Copies.

  You may convey verbatim copies of the Program's source code as you
receive it, in any medium, provided that you conspicuously and
appropriately publish on each copy an appropriate copyright notice;
keep intact all notices stating that this License and any
non-permissive terms added in accord with section 7 apply to the code;
keep intact all notices of the absence of any warranty; and give all
recipients a copy of this License along with the Program.

  You may charge any price or no price for each copy that you convey,
and you may offer support or warranty protection for a fee.

  5. Conveying Modified Source Versions.

  You may convey a work based on the Program, or the modifications to
produce it from the Program, in the form of source code under the
terms of section 4, provided that you also meet all of these conditions:

```

```
    a) The work must carry prominent notices stating that you modified
    it, and giving a relevant date.

    b) The work must carry prominent notices stating that it is
    released under this License and any conditions added under section
    7.  This requirement modifies the requirement in section 4 to
    "keep intact all notices".

    c) You must license the entire work, as a whole, under this
    License to anyone who comes into possession of a copy.  This
    License will therefore apply, along with any applicable section 7
    additional terms, to the whole of the work, and all its parts,
    regardless of how they are packaged.  This License gives no
    permission to license the work in any other way, but it does not
    invalidate such permission if you have separately received it.

    d) If the work has interactive user interfaces, each must display
    Appropriate Legal Notices; however, if the Program has interactive
    interfaces that do not display Appropriate Legal Notices, your
    work need not make them do so.

  A compilation of a covered work with other separate and independent
works, which are not by their nature extensions of the covered work,
and which are not combined with it such as to form a larger program,
in or on a volume of a storage or distribution medium, is called an
"aggregate" if the compilation and its resulting copyright are not
used to limit the access or legal rights of the compilation's users
beyond what the individual works permit.  Inclusion of a covered work
in an aggregate does not cause this License to apply to the other
parts of the aggregate.

  6. Conveying Non-Source Forms.

  You may convey a covered work in object code form under the terms
of sections 4 and 5, provided that you also convey the
machine-readable Corresponding Source under the terms of this License,
in one of these ways:

    a) Convey the object code in, or embodied in, a physical product
    (including a physical distribution medium), accompanied by the
    Corresponding Source fixed on a durable physical medium
    customarily used for software interchange.

    b) Convey the object code in, or embodied in, a physical product
    (including a physical distribution medium), accompanied by a
    written offer, valid for at least three years and valid for as
    long as you offer spare parts or customer support for that product
    model, to give anyone who possesses the object code either (1) a
    copy of the Corresponding Source for all the software in the
    product that is covered by this License, on a durable physical
    medium customarily used for software interchange, for a price no
    more than your reasonable cost of physically performing this
    conveying of source, or (2) access to copy the
    Corresponding Source from a network server at no charge.
```

```

    c) Convey individual copies of the object code with a copy of the
    written offer to provide the Corresponding Source.  This
    alternative is allowed only occasionally and noncommercially, and
    only if you received the object code with such an offer, in accord
    with subsection 6b.

    d) Convey the object code by offering access from a designated
    place (gratis or for a charge), and offer equivalent access to the
    Corresponding Source in the same way through the same place at no
    further charge.  You need not require recipients to copy the
    Corresponding Source along with the object code.  If the place to
    copy the object code is a network server, the Corresponding Source
    may be on a different server (operated by you or a third party)
    that supports equivalent copying facilities, provided you maintain
    clear directions next to the object code saying where to find the
    Corresponding Source.  Regardless of what server hosts the
    Corresponding Source, you remain obligated to ensure that it is
    available for as long as needed to satisfy these requirements.

    e) Convey the object code using peer-to-peer transmission, provided
    you inform other peers where the object code and Corresponding
    Source of the work are being offered to the general public at no
    charge under subsection 6d.

  A separable portion of the object code, whose source code is excluded
from the Corresponding Source as a System Library, need not be
included in conveying the object code work.

  A "User Product" is either (1) a "consumer product", which means any
tangible personal property which is normally used for personal, family,
or household purposes, or (2) anything designed or sold for incorporation
into a dwelling.  In determining whether a product is a consumer product,
doubtful cases shall be resolved in favor of coverage.  For a particular
product received by a particular user, "normally used" refers to a
typical or common use of that class of product, regardless of the status
of the particular user or of the way in which the particular user
actually uses, or expects or is expected to use, the product.  A product
is a consumer product regardless of whether the product has substantial
commercial, industrial or non-consumer uses, unless such uses represent
the only significant mode of use of the product.

  "Installation Information" for a User Product means any methods,
procedures, authorization keys, or other information required to install
and execute modified versions of a covered work in that User Product from
a modified version of its Corresponding Source.  The information must
suffice to ensure that the continued functioning of the modified object
code is in no case prevented or interfered with solely because
modification has been made.

  If you convey an object code work under this section in, or with, or
specifically for use in, a User Product, and the conveying occurs as
part of a transaction in which the right of possession and use of the
User Product is transferred to the recipient in perpetuity or for a
```

```
fixed term (regardless of how the transaction is characterized), the
Corresponding Source conveyed under this section must be accompanied
by the Installation Information.  But this requirement does not apply
if neither you nor any third party retains the ability to install
modified object code on the User Product (for example, the work has
been installed in ROM).

  The requirement to provide Installation Information does not include a
requirement to continue to provide support service, warranty, or updates
for a work that has been modified or installed by the recipient, or for
the User Product in which it has been modified or installed.  Access to a
network may be denied when the modification itself materially and
adversely affects the operation of the network or violates the rules and
protocols for communication across the network.

  Corresponding Source conveyed, and Installation Information provided,
in accord with this section must be in a format that is publicly
documented (and with an implementation available to the public in
source code form), and must require no special password or key for
unpacking, reading or copying.

  7. Additional Terms.

  "Additional permissions" are terms that supplement the terms of this
License by making exceptions from one or more of its conditions.
Additional permissions that are applicable to the entire Program shall
be treated as though they were included in this License, to the extent
that they are valid under applicable law.  If additional permissions
apply only to part of the Program, that part may be used separately
under those permissions, but the entire Program remains governed by
this License without regard to the additional permissions.

  When you convey a copy of a covered work, you may at your option
remove any additional permissions from that copy, or from any part of
it.  (Additional permissions may be written to require their own
removal in certain cases when you modify the work.)  You may place
additional permissions on material, added by you to a covered work,
for which you have or can give appropriate copyright permission.

  Notwithstanding any other provision of this License, for material you
add to a covered work, you may (if authorized by the copyright holders of
that material) supplement the terms of this License with terms:

    a) Disclaiming warranty or limiting liability differently from the
    terms of sections 15 and 16 of this License; or

    b) Requiring preservation of specified reasonable legal notices or
    author attributions in that material or in the Appropriate Legal
    Notices displayed by works containing it; or

    c) Prohibiting misrepresentation of the origin of that material, or
    requiring that modified versions of such material be marked in
    reasonable ways as different from the original version; or

```

```
    d) Limiting the use for publicity purposes of names of licensors or
    authors of the material; or

    e) Declining to grant rights under trademark law for use of some
    trade names, trademarks, or service marks; or

    f) Requiring indemnification of licensors and authors of that
    material by anyone who conveys the material (or modified versions of
    it) with contractual assumptions of liability to the recipient, for
    any liability that these contractual assumptions directly impose on
    those licensors and authors.

  All other non-permissive additional terms are considered "further
restrictions" within the meaning of section 10.  If the Program as you
received it, or any part of it, contains a notice stating that it is
governed by this License along with a term that is a further
restriction, you may remove that term.  If a license document contains
a further restriction but permits relicensing or conveying under this
License, you may add to a covered work material governed by the terms
of that license document, provided that the further restriction does
not survive such relicensing or conveying.

  If you add terms to a covered work in accord with this section, you
must place, in the relevant source files, a statement of the
additional terms that apply to those files, or a notice indicating
where to find the applicable terms.

  Additional terms, permissive or non-permissive, may be stated in the
form of a separately written license, or stated as exceptions;
the above requirements apply either way.

  8. Termination.

  You may not propagate or modify a covered work except as expressly
provided under this License.  Any attempt otherwise to propagate or
modify it is void, and will automatically terminate your rights under
this License (including any patent licenses granted under the third
paragraph of section 11).

  However, if you cease all violation of this License, then your
license from a particular copyright holder is reinstated (a)
provisionally, unless and until the copyright holder explicitly and
finally terminates your license, and (b) permanently, if the copyright
holder fails to notify you of the violation by some reasonable means
prior to 60 days after the cessation.

  Moreover, your license from a particular copyright holder is
reinstated permanently if the copyright holder notifies you of the
violation by some reasonable means, this is the first time you have
received notice of violation of this License (for any work) from that
copyright holder, and you cure the violation prior to 30 days after
your receipt of the notice.

  Termination of your rights under this section does not terminate the
```

```
licenses of parties who have received copies or rights from you under
this License.  If your rights have been terminated and not permanently
reinstated, you do not qualify to receive new licenses for the same
material under section 10.

  9. Acceptance Not Required for Having Copies.

  You are not required to accept this License in order to receive or
run a copy of the Program.  Ancillary propagation of a covered work
occurring solely as a consequence of using peer-to-peer transmission
to receive a copy likewise does not require acceptance.  However,
nothing other than this License grants you permission to propagate or
modify any covered work.  These actions infringe copyright if you do
not accept this License.  Therefore, by modifying or propagating a
covered work, you indicate your acceptance of this License to do so.

  10. Automatic Licensing of Downstream Recipients.

  Each time you convey a covered work, the recipient automatically
receives a license from the original licensors, to run, modify and
propagate that work, subject to this License.  You are not responsible
for enforcing compliance by third parties with this License.

  An "entity transaction" is a transaction transferring control of an
organization, or substantially all assets of one, or subdividing an
organization, or merging organizations.  If propagation of a covered
work results from an entity transaction, each party to that
transaction who receives a copy of the work also receives whatever
licenses to the work the party's predecessor in interest had or could
give under the previous paragraph, plus a right to possession of the
Corresponding Source of the work from the predecessor in interest, if
the predecessor has it or can get it with reasonable efforts.

  You may not impose any further restrictions on the exercise of the
rights granted or affirmed under this License.  For example, you may
not impose a license fee, royalty, or other charge for exercise of
rights granted under this License, and you may not initiate litigation
(including a cross-claim or counterclaim in a lawsuit) alleging that
any patent claim is infringed by making, using, selling, offering for
sale, or importing the Program or any portion of it.

  11. Patents.

  A "contributor" is a copyright holder who authorizes use under this
License of the Program or a work on which the Program is based.  The
work thus licensed is called the contributor's "contributor version".

  A contributor's "essential patent claims" are all patent claims
owned or controlled by the contributor, whether already acquired or
hereafter acquired, that would be infringed by some manner, permitted
by this License, of making, using, or selling its contributor version,
but do not include claims that would be infringed only as a
consequence of further modification of the contributor version.  For
purposes of this definition, "control" includes the right to grant
```

```
patent sublicenses in a manner consistent with the requirements of
this License.

  Each contributor grants you a non-exclusive, worldwide, royalty-free
patent license under the contributor's essential patent claims, to
make, use, sell, offer for sale, import and otherwise run, modify and
propagate the contents of its contributor version.

  In the following three paragraphs, a "patent license" is any express
agreement or commitment, however denominated, not to enforce a patent
(such as an express permission to practice a patent or covenant not to
sue for patent infringement).  To "grant" such a patent license to a
party means to make such an agreement or commitment not to enforce a
patent against the party.

  If you convey a covered work, knowingly relying on a patent license,
and the Corresponding Source of the work is not available for anyone
to copy, free of charge and under the terms of this License, through a
publicly available network server or other readily accessible means,
then you must either (1) cause the Corresponding Source to be so
available, or (2) arrange to deprive yourself of the benefit of the
patent license for this particular work, or (3) arrange, in a manner
consistent with the requirements of this License, to extend the patent
license to downstream recipients.  "Knowingly relying" means you have
actual knowledge that, but for the patent license, your conveying the
covered work in a country, or your recipient's use of the covered work
in a country, would infringe one or more identifiable patents in that
country that you have reason to believe are valid.

  If, pursuant to or in connection with a single transaction or
arrangement, you convey, or propagate by procuring conveyance of, a
covered work, and grant a patent license to some of the parties
receiving the covered work authorizing them to use, propagate, modify
or convey a specific copy of the covered work, then the patent license
you grant is automatically extended to all recipients of the covered
work and works based on it.

  A patent license is "discriminatory" if it does not include within
the scope of its coverage, prohibits the exercise of, or is
conditioned on the non-exercise of one or more of the rights that are
specifically granted under this License.  You may not convey a covered
work if you are a party to an arrangement with a third party that is
in the business of distributing software, under which you make payment
to the third party based on the extent of your activity of conveying
the work, and under which the third party grants, to any of the
parties who would receive the covered work from you, a discriminatory
patent license (a) in connection with copies of the covered work
conveyed by you (or copies made from those copies), or (b) primarily
for and in connection with specific products or compilations that
contain the covered work, unless you entered into that arrangement,
or that patent license was granted, prior to 28 March 2007.

  Nothing in this License shall be construed as excluding or limiting
any implied license or other defenses to infringement that may
```

```
otherwise be available to you under applicable patent law.

  12. No Surrender of Others' Freedom.

  If conditions are imposed on you (whether by court order, agreement or
otherwise) that contradict the conditions of this License, they do not
excuse you from the conditions of this License.  If you cannot convey a
covered work so as to satisfy simultaneously your obligations under this
License and any other pertinent obligations, then as a consequence you may
not convey it at all.  For example, if you agree to terms that obligate
you
to collect a royalty for further conveying from those to whom you convey
the Program, the only way you could satisfy both those terms and this
License would be to refrain entirely from conveying the Program.

  13. Use with the GNU Affero General Public License.

  Notwithstanding any other provision of this License, you have
permission to link or combine any covered work with a work licensed
under version 3 of the GNU Affero General Public License into a single
combined work, and to convey the resulting work.  The terms of this
License will continue to apply to the part which is the covered work,
but the special requirements of the GNU Affero General Public License,
section 13, concerning interaction through a network will apply to the
combination as such.

  14. Revised Versions of this License.

  The Free Software Foundation may publish revised and/or new versions of
the GNU General Public License from time to time.  Such new versions will
be similar in spirit to the present version, but may differ in detail to
address new problems or concerns.

  Each version is given a distinguishing version number.  If the
Program specifies that a certain numbered version of the GNU General
Public License "or any later version" applies to it, you have the
option of following the terms and conditions either of that numbered
version or of any later version published by the Free Software
Foundation.  If the Program does not specify a version number of the
GNU General Public License, you may choose any version ever published
by the Free Software Foundation.

  If the Program specifies that a proxy can decide which future
versions of the GNU General Public License can be used, that proxy's
public statement of acceptance of a version permanently authorizes you
to choose that version for the Program.

  Later license versions may give you additional or different
permissions.  However, no additional obligations are imposed on any
author or copyright holder as a result of your choosing to follow a
later version.

  15. Disclaimer of Warranty.

```

```
  THERE IS NO WARRANTY FOR THE PROGRAM, TO THE EXTENT PERMITTED BY
APPLICABLE LAW.  EXCEPT WHEN OTHERWISE STATED IN WRITING THE COPYRIGHT
HOLDERS AND/OR OTHER PARTIES PROVIDE THE PROGRAM "AS IS" WITHOUT WARRANTY
OF ANY KIND, EITHER EXPRESSED OR IMPLIED, INCLUDING, BUT NOT LIMITED TO,
THE IMPLIED WARRANTIES OF MERCHANTABILITY AND FITNESS FOR A PARTICULAR
PURPOSE.  THE ENTIRE RISK AS TO THE QUALITY AND PERFORMANCE OF THE PROGRAM
IS WITH YOU.  SHOULD THE PROGRAM PROVE DEFECTIVE, YOU ASSUME THE COST OF
ALL NECESSARY SERVICING, REPAIR OR CORRECTION.

  16. Limitation of Liability.

  IN NO EVENT UNLESS REQUIRED BY APPLICABLE LAW OR AGREED TO IN WRITING
WILL ANY COPYRIGHT HOLDER, OR ANY OTHER PARTY WHO MODIFIES AND/OR CONVEYS
THE PROGRAM AS PERMITTED ABOVE, BE LIABLE TO YOU FOR DAMAGES, INCLUDING ANY
GENERAL, SPECIAL, INCIDENTAL OR CONSEQUENTIAL DAMAGES ARISING OUT OF THE
USE OR INABILITY TO USE THE PROGRAM (INCLUDING BUT NOT LIMITED TO LOSS OF
DATA OR DATA BEING RENDERED INACCURATE OR LOSSES SUSTAINED BY YOU OR THIRD
PARTIES OR A FAILURE OF THE PROGRAM TO OPERATE WITH ANY OTHER PROGRAMS),
EVEN IF SUCH HOLDER OR OTHER PARTY HAS BEEN ADVISED OF THE POSSIBILITY OF
SUCH DAMAGES.

  17. Interpretation of Sections 15 and 16.

  If the disclaimer of warranty and limitation of liability provided
above cannot be given local legal effect according to their terms,
reviewing courts shall apply local law that most closely approximates
an absolute waiver of all civil liability in connection with the
Program, unless a warranty or assumption of liability accompanies a
copy of the Program in return for a fee.

                     END OF TERMS AND CONDITIONS

            How to Apply These Terms to Your New Programs

  If you develop a new program, and you want it to be of the greatest
possible use to the public, the best way to achieve this is to make it
free software which everyone can redistribute and change under these terms.

  To do so, attach the following notices to the program.  It is safest
to attach them to the start of each source file to most effectively
state the exclusion of warranty; and each file should have at least
the "copyright" line and a pointer to where the full notice is found.

    <one line to give the program's name and a brief idea of what it does.>
    Copyright (C) <year>  <name of author>

    This program is free software: you can redistribute it and/or modify
    it under the terms of the GNU General Public License as published by
    the Free Software Foundation, either version 3 of the License, or
    (at your option) any later version.

```

```
    This program is distributed in the hope that it will be useful,
    but WITHOUT ANY WARRANTY; without even the implied warranty of
    MERCHANTABILITY or FITNESS FOR A PARTICULAR PURPOSE.  See the
    GNU General Public License for more details.

    You should have received a copy of the GNU General Public License
    along with this program.  If not, see <http://www.gnu.org/licenses/>.

Also add information on how to contact you by electronic and paper mail.

  If the program does terminal interaction, make it output a short
notice like this when it starts in an interactive mode:

    <program>  Copyright (C) <year>  <name of author>
    This program comes with ABSOLUTELY NO WARRANTY; for details type 'show w'.
    This is free software, and you are welcome to redistribute it
    under certain conditions; type 'show c' for details.

The hypothetical commands 'show w' and 'show c' should show the appropriate
parts of the General Public License.  Of course, your program's commands
might be different; for a GUI interface, you would use an "about box".

  You should also get your employer (if you work as a programmer) or school,
if any, to sign a "copyright disclaimer" for the program, if necessary.
For more information on this, and how to apply and follow the GNU GPL, see
<http://www.gnu.org/licenses/>.

  The GNU General Public License does not permit incorporating your program
into proprietary programs.  If your program is a subroutine library, you
may consider it more useful to permit linking proprietary applications with
the library.  If this is what you want to do, use the GNU Lesser General
Public License instead of this License.  But first, please read
<http://www.gnu.org/philosophy/why-not-lgpl.html>.
```

4.4.2 kybyz_v0/Makefile

Listing 4.33: kybyz_v0/Makefile

```
ST := California
L := Petaluma
O := Unternet
E := hostmaster
OU := Tech
DRYRUN ?= --dry-run
all: restart
localtest: kybyz.py
	python $<
client_test: localtest
	wget -O- --quiet http://kybyz0:2424
%.key: Makefile
	openssl genrsa -out $@ 1024
%.csr: %.key
	n=$(notdir $*) && \
	cn=www.$(notdir $*) && \
	openssl req -new -key $< -out $@ -subj \
	 /C=US/ST=$(ST)/L=$(L)/O=$(O)/OU=$(OU)/CN=$$cn/emailAddress=$(E)@$$n
%.crt: %.csr
	openssl x509 -req -days 365 -in $< -signkey $*.key -out $@
%.private.pem: Makefile
	openssl genrsa -out $@ 4096
	openssl rsa -text -in $@
%.public.pem: %.private.pem
	openssl rsa -pubout -in $< -out $@
	openssl rsa -text -pubin -in $@
.PRECIOUS: %.key %.csr %.private.pem
$(HOME)/etc/kybyz0:
	mkdir -p $@
keys:	$(HOME)/etc/kybyz0
	$(MAKE) $</kybyz.crt
	$(MAKE) $</kybyz.public.pem
$(USER)-kybyz.ini: client.ini.template
	envsubst < $< > $@
kybyz-example.ini: example.ini.template
	envsubst < $< > $@
ini: $(USER)-kybyz.ini kybyz-example.ini
	cwd=$(PWD); for file in $+; do \
	 (cd /etc/uwsgi/apps-enabled && sudo ln -sf $$cwd/$$file .); \
	done
restart: $(USER)-kybyz.ini $(HOME)/.kybyz_v0/favicon.ico
	uwsgi $<
backup:
	for server in backup1 backup2; do \
	 rsync -avuz $(DRYRUN) --delete ~/.kybyz/ $$server:.kybyz/; \
	done
%/favicon.ico: %
	convert -background none -fill green \
	 -size 128x128 -gravity center \
	 -font Helvetica label:k png:- | \
```

```
        convert - -bordercolor white -border 0 \
        \( -clone 0 -resize '16x16!' \) \
        \( -clone 0 -resize '32x32!' \) \
        \( -clone 0 -resize '48x48!' \) \
        \( -clone 0 -resize '64x64!' \) \
        -delete 0 -alpha off -colors 256 -transparent white $@
%.pylint: %.py
        pylint $<
pylint: kybyz.pylint
%.doctest: %.py
        python3 -mdoctest --verbose $<
doctests: kybyz.doctest
.FORCE:
```

4.4.3 kybyz_v0/README.md

Listing 4.34: kybyz_v0/README.md

```
# kybyz
kibitzing website, facebook-killer. what my "goals" idea was supposed
to be but never materialized.

ideas: everything shareable, commentable, thumbs-up, thumbs-down,
whatever. use unicode glyphs rather than graphics for icons. make
everything pure html for those who want it, add web2 stuff for those
who enable javascript. everybody posts in markdown.

other ideas: everything takes place on one's own machine. app for
smartphones and tablets. server only acts as temporary cache. all
uploads to server encrypted with uploader's public key except for
sender and recipient, which are the lower half of the entities'
public keys. should also be encrypted with recipient's public key,
especially for private messages, perhaps not default for posts sent
to multiple recipients. once a public key has been shared with that
many recipients the expectation of privacy drops to near-zero.

not keeping server logs will make it impossible for agencies
to get any data.

can tweet kybyzym to other adopters by using hashtag #kybyz
followed by enough letters of message hash to make it unique to
that adopter, followed by the one-character icon plus the text.
it is fetched through twitter API periodically by client programs.

more thoughts as posted on Fb: https://www.facebook.com/
jcomeauictx/posts/10155975677545615?pnref=story

maybe can use IPOP (http://ipop-project.org/) VPNs for peer-to-peer
connectivity.
```

4.4.4 kybyz_v0/client.ini.template

Listing 4.35: kybyz_v0/client.ini.template

```
[uwsgi]
# symlink this under /etc/uwsgi/apps-enabled/ (Debian)
#log-syslog
http-socket = kybyz0:2424
plugin = python3
wsgi-file = $PWD/kybyz.py
callable = kybyz_client
chdir = $PWD
uid = $USER
check-static = /home/$USER/.kybyz_v0
# do not load `site` module while root, load it later as user
no-site
# log already created, no need for following
#logto = /var/log/uwsgi/app/%n.log
# guide to "magic" variables:
# http://uwsgi-docs.readthedocs.io/en/latest/Configuration.html
```

4.4.5 kybyz_v0/example.ini.template

Listing 4.36: kybyz_v0/example.ini.template

```
[uwsgi]
# symlink this under /etc/uwsgi/apps-enabled/ (Debian)
#log-syslog
http-socket = kybyz0:2727
plugin = python
wsgi-file = $PWD/kybyz.py
callable = example_client
chdir = $PWD
check-static = $PWD/example.kybyz
uid = $USER
# do not load `site` module while root, load it later as user
no-site
#logto = /var/log/uwsgi/app/%n.log
# guide to "magic" variables:
# http://uwsgi-docs.readthedocs.io/en/latest/Configuration.html
```

4.4.6 kybyz_v0/kybyz.py

Listing 4.37: kybyz_v0/kybyz.py

```
#!/usr/bin/python3
'''
implement local website http://kybyz/

Copyright 2015-2016 John Otis Comeau <jc@unternet.net>
distributed under the terms of the GNU General Public License Version 3
(see COPYING)

automatically uploads to and downloads from kybyz.com to populate the
local website.

must first mate a local IP address with the name 'kybyz0' in /etc/hosts, e.g.:

127.0.1.125 kybyz0
'''
from __future__ import print_function
import sys, os, logging, pwd, subprocess, site, cgi, html
site.main()
logging.basicConfig(level=logging.DEBUG if __debug__ else logging.INFO)
logging.debug('os.getuid(): %s', os.getuid())
logging.debug('os.geteuid(): %s', os.geteuid())
logging.debug('site.ENABLE_USER_SITE: %s', site.ENABLE_USER_SITE)
logging.debug('site.USER_SITE: %s', site.USER_SITE)
logging.debug('sys.path: %s', sys.path)
import rsa
from markdown import markdown
try:  # command-line testing won't have module available
    import uwsgi
except ImportError:
    uwsgi = type('uwsgi', (), {'opt': {}})  # object with empty opt attribute
logging.debug('uwsgi.opt: %s' % repr(uwsgi.opt))
MAXLENGTH = 1024 * 1024  # maximum size in bytes of markdown source of post
HOMEDIR = pwd.getpwuid(os.getuid()).pw_dir
DATADIR = uwsgi.opt.get('check_static', os.path.join(HOMEDIR, '.kybyz_v0'))
THISDIR = os.path.dirname(sys.argv[0]) or os.path.abspath('.')
EXAMPLE = uwsgi.opt.get('check_static', os.path.join(THISDIR, 'example.kybyz'))
logging.debug('HOMEDIR: %s' % HOMEDIR)
logging.debug('USER_SITE: %s' % site.USER_SITE)
USER_CONFIG = os.path.join(HOMEDIR, 'etc', 'kybyz0')
PRIVATE_KEY = os.path.join(USER_CONFIG, 'kybyz.private.pem')
PUBLIC_KEY = os.path.join(USER_CONFIG, 'kybyz.public.pem')
MIMETYPES = {'png': 'image/png', 'ico': 'image/x-icon', 'jpg': 'image/jpeg',
             'jpeg': 'image/jpeg', 'pdf': 'application/pdf'}
FILETYPES = [
    'directory',
```

```
    'md',
    'url',
    'txt',
    'html',
    'css',
] + list(MIMETYPES.keys())

class Node(str):
    '''
    a Node is either a category or an action item (goal, task, etc.)

    nodes must be named as follows:

    if a directory, it can be a singleton, e.g. '.kybyz' or 'goals'
    it can also be a word followed by an attribute, e.g. 'jogging.accomplished'

    if a file, it can be in two or 3 parts.
    the final part should always be a filetype, e.g. 'jogging.html'
    a middle part can be added as an attribute, e.g. 'house.accomplished.md'
    '''
    # class attributes
    root = None  # filled in during __init__()

    def __new__(cls, parent_node, filename):
        '''
        create a new Node object
        '''
        parts = os.path.basename(filename).split('.')
        name = parts[0]  # .kybyz will be ''
        # obviously there can be only one .hidden name in a directory
        try:
            siblings = parent_node.attributes['children']
        except (KeyError, AttributeError):
            siblings = []
        if name in siblings:
            logging.info('Returning pre-existing node %s', name)
            node = siblings[siblings.index(name)]
        else:
            node = super(Node, cls).__new__(cls, name)
        return node

    def __init__(self, parent_node, filename):
        '''
        initialize the current node, which may have already been initialized

        so we can't just assume, e.g., that we can set self.children = []

        names must be in 2 or 3 parts, e.g.:

        mygoal.md: a markdown file for "mygoal"
        mygoal.accomplished: a directory for accomplishments of mygoal
```

```
        mygoal.related.md: a file for other nodes related to "mygoal"
        '''
        logging.debug('Node.__init__(%s, %s)', parent_node, filename)
        parts = os.path.basename(filename).split('.')
        self.filename = filename
        self.attributes = {}
        self.name = parts[0]
        attribute = parts[1] if len(parts) > 1 else None
        filetype = 'directory' if os.path.isdir(filename) else parts[-1]
        if parent_node is None:
            attribute = None
            if not os.path.isdir(filename):
                raise(AttributeError('root filename must be directory'))
            filetype = 'directory'
            Node.root = self  # set class attribute
            self.parent = self
            self.attributes['children'] = self.attributes.get('children', [])
            logging.debug('initialized root node')
        elif os.path.isdir(filename):
            self.parent = parent_node
            if not self in parent_node.attributes['children']:
                parent_node.attributes['children'].append(self)
            self.attributes['children'] = self.attributes.get('children', [])
        else:
            self.parent = parent_node
            if not self in parent_node.attributes['children']:
                parent_node.attributes['children'].append(self)
        if filetype not in FILETYPES:
            if attribute != filetype:
                raise(ValueError('Unknown filetype: "%s"' % filetype))
            elif not os.path.isdir(filename):
                logging.error('%s does not have filetype extension', filename)
                raise(TypeError('Path without extension must be directory'))
            else:
                attribute = None  # e.g. running.md or mygoal.html
        if attribute and filetype == 'directory':
            files = listdir(filename)
            header, trailer = None, None
            if 'header.html' in files:
                header = files.pop(files.index('header.html'))
            if 'trailer.html' in files:
                trailer = files.pop(files.index('trailer.html'))
            self.attributes[attribute] = []
            if header:
                self.attributes[attribute].append(render(header))
            self.attributes[attribute].extend([render(f)[0] for f in files])
            if trailer:
                self.attributes[attribute].append(render(trailer))
        elif attribute:
```

```
                self.attributes[attribute] = [render(filename)[0]]
            if parent_node is None:
                self.root = self  # class attribute
                self.parent = self

def kybyz_client(env = None, start_response = None):
    '''
    primary client process, shows contents of $HOME/.kybyz_v0
    '''
    logging.debug('env: %s' % repr(env))
    start = DATADIR
    logging.debug('start: %s' % start)
    private, public = load_keys()
    path = (env.get('HTTP_PATH', env.get('REQUEST_URI', '/'))).lstrip('/')
    if not path:
        mimetype = 'text/html'
        page = makepage(start, [], [])
    else:
        page, mimetype = render(path)
        logging.debug('mimetype: %s', mimetype)
    start_response('200 groovy', [('Content-type', mimetype)])
    return page

def example_client(env = None, start_response = None):
    '''
    testing client process, shows contents of $PWD/example.kybyz/
    '''
    logging.debug('env: %s', repr(env))
    start = EXAMPLE
    logging.debug('start: %s', start)
    private, public = load_keys()
    path = (env.get('HTTP_PATH', env.get('REQUEST_URI', '/'))).lstrip('/')
    if not path:
        mimetype = 'text/html'
        page = buildpage(start)
    else:
        page, mimetype = render(path)
    start_response('200 groovy', [('Content-type', mimetype)])
    return [page]

def listdir(directory):
    '''
    os.listdir() but returns full path of each file
    '''
    return [os.path.join(directory, f) for f in os.listdir(directory)]

def pushdir(stack, directory):
    '''
    implementation of MSDOS `pushd`
    '''
    stack.append(directory)
    logging.debug('stack after `pushdir` now: %s' % stack)
    os.chdir(directory)

```

```
def popdir(stack):
    '''
    implementation of MSDOS `popd`
    '''
    stack.pop(-1)
    logging.debug('stack after `popdir` now: %s'% stack)
    os.chdir('..')

def render(pagename):
    '''
    Return content with Content-type header

    If it's markdown, we assume it's a post and will wrap it with
    <div class="post">, but if it's HTML we can't assume anything as
    it could be the header or footer or something else. So if you're using
    HTML for a post, wrap it yourself.
    '''
    if pagename.endswith('.md'):
        logging.debug('running markdown on %s', pagename)
        return postwrap(markdown(read(pagename),
                      extensions=['fenced_code']).encode()), 'text/html'
    elif pagename.endswith('.html'):
        logging.debug('rendering %s as html', pagename)
        return read(pagename, raw=True), 'text/html'
    elif not pagename.endswith(('.pdf', '.png', '.ico', '.jpg', '.jpeg')):
        logging.debug('rendering %s as plain text', pagename)
        return ('<div class="post">%s</div>' % html.escape(
            read(pagename)).encode(), 'text/plain')
    else:
        # we don't want pdf and image files cluttering the page
        logging.debug('skipping resource %s', pagename)
        # using string '' will cause uwsgi
        # ERROR: Unhandled object from iterator
        # and the content will not show
        return ('', 'text/html')

def buildpage(directory=DATADIR):
    '''
    Rewrite of `makepage` using Node

    Note that this constructs Nodes out of the same path more than once,
    which is why Node.__new__ has to return an existing node when found.
    '''
    parent = None
    page = ''
    for dirpath, dirnames, filenames in os.walk(directory):
        node = Node(parent, dirpath)
        parent = node
        for entry in dirnames + filenames:
            subnode = Node(parent, os.path.join(dirpath, entry))
    for node in walk(Node.root):
        logging.debug('node: %r', node[:50])
        page += str(node)
    return page
```

```

def walk(node):
    '''
    Like os.walk, but for Node objects

    http://stackoverflow.com/a/3010038/493161
    '''
    yield node
    for attribute in getattr(node, 'attributes', {}):
        for child in node.attributes[attribute]:
            for entry in walk(child):
                yield entry

def makepage(directory=DATADIR, output=None, level=None):
    '''
    Scan folders and files to build the Kybyz page
    '''
    logging.debug('running `makepage` on %s' % directory)
    output, level = output if output else [], level if level else []
    pushdir(level, directory)
    posts = specialsort(os.listdir('.'))
    logging.debug('posts: %s' % posts)
    for post in posts:
        page = []
        if post.startswith('.'):
            '''
            files and directories with a special meaning
            '''
            if post.startswith('.accomplished'):
                '''
                an '.accomplished' *directory* means it contains steps to
                accomplishment; an '.accomplished' *file* means it is *done*.
                '''
                if os.path.isdir(post):
                    logging.debug('task %s has accomplishment activity',
                                  level[-1])
                else:
                    logging.debug('goal %s has been accomplished', level[-1])
                page.append('&#x2713;')
        elif not os.path.isdir(post):
            page.append(render(post)[0])
        else:
            headerlevel = len(level) + 1 # <h2> and higher
            page.append(postwrap(True))
            page.append('<h%d>%s</h%d>' % (headerlevel, post, headerlevel))
            page += makepage(post, [], level)
            page.append(postwrap(False))
        logging.debug('page: "%s"', page)
        output += page
    logging.debug('output: "%r"', output)
    popdir(level)
```

```
    return output

def postwrap(something):
    '''
    Encapsulate post in DIV tags.

    Works one-shot with a string, or in 2 steps by passing in True (open)
    or False (close)
    '''
    if isinstance(something, int):  # expecting True (1) or False (0)
        return [b'</div>', b'<div class="post">'][something]
    else:
        return b'<div class="post">%s</div>' % something

def specialsort(listing):
    '''
    sort files first, then subdirectories

    (and/or any other method that makes sense as we progress
    note that symlinks will also be identified properly as files or dirs
    '''
    subdirs = list(filter(os.path.isdir, listing))
    files = list(filter(os.path.isfile, listing))
    if set(listing) != set(subdirs + files):
        raise ValueError('%s != %s' % (listing, subdirs + files))
    return sorted(files) + sorted(subdirs)

def read(filename, maxread = MAXLENGTH, raw=False):
    '''
    return contents of a file, closing it properly
    '''
    decoded = None
    try:
        infile = open(filename, 'rb')
        data = infile.read(MAXLENGTH)
        infile.close()
        if not raw:
            try:
                decoded = data.decode('utf8')
            except UnicodeDecodeError:
                decoded = data.decode('latin1')
    except IOError:
        message = ('File %s was not found relative to %s' %
                   (filename, os.path.abspath(os.curdir)))
        logging.error(message)
        decoded = message
    return decoded or data

def load_keys():
    '''
    load client keys, aborting if not already created

    note: key creation takes *forever* (or overnight anyway) on a slow
    computer. if you have openssl installed, use the Makefile to
```

```
    'make keys'
    '''
    try:
        private = rsa.PrivateKey.load_pkcs1(read(PRIVATE_KEY))
    except IOError:
        raise Exception('First create keys using `make kybyz.public.key`')
    try:
        public = rsa.PublicKey.load_pkcs1(read(PUBLIC_KEY))
    except ValueError:
        public = rsa.PublicKey.load_pkcs1_openssl_pem(read(PUBLIC_KEY))
    return private, public

if __name__ == '__main__':
    print('\n'.join(example_client(os.environ, lambda *args: None)))

# vim: tabstop=8 expandtab shiftwidth=4 softtabstop=4
```

4.5 Subdirectory kybyz_v0/example.kybyz/

4.5.1 kybyz_v0/example.kybyz/header.html

Listing 4.38: kybyz_v0/example.kybyz/header.html

```
<!doctype html>
<html lang="en">
<head>
  <meta charset="utf-8">
  <title>Kybyz Homepage</title>
  <link rel="stylesheet" type="text/css" href="kybyz.css">
</head>
<body>
```

4.5.2 kybyz_v0/example.kybyz/homepage.md

Listing 4.39: kybyz_v0/example.kybyz/homepage.md

```
## This is the post header. If deleted, the directory name will be used
as header.
This is my `kybyz` homepage, written in `markdown` language. This line
following the header is the "summary", or "short description" of the post.
If there is no single line ending with a period here, a fragment of the
remaining text, the "body" of the post, will be used instead, followed
by an ellipsis.

Copy this entire example.kybyz directory to your own home directory, e.g.:
`cp -a example.kybyz ~/.kybyz`, and edit the files as you wish, adding other
files and directories to personalize it.

`This is some long-assed text and I want to find out if it wraps like it's supposed to, or if I screwed up the css somehow. But I have to make this long enough to exceed the screen width, and I'm not sure how much that will take. Let's see if this works.`

`I also want to find out if allthistextwithnospaceswillwrapIdoubtitwillbutwhoknowsnothingisimpossibleexcepti
`
```

4.5.3 kybyz_v0/example.kybyz/kybyz.css

Listing 4.40: kybyz_v0/example.kybyz/kybyz.css

```
div.post {
        border: 1px solid black;
        padding: 1em;
}
body {
        overflow-wrap: break-word;
}
pre, code {
        white-space: pre-wrap;
}
```

4.5.4 kybyz_v0/example.kybyz/trailer.html

Listing 4.41: kybyz_v0/example.kybyz/trailer.html

```
</body>
</html>
```

4.6 Subdirectory resources/

4.6.1 resources/.gitignore

Listing 4.42: resources/.gitignore

```
vis-network.min.js
```